180
PRAYERS TO
Help You
Sleep

© 2023 by Barbour Publishing, Inc.

Print ISBN 978-1-63609-617-9

Published by Barbour Publishing, Inc., 1810 Barbour Drive, Uhrichsville, Ohio 44683, www.barbourbooks.com

Our mission is to inspire the world with the life-changing message of the Bible.

Member of the
Evangelical Christian
Publishers Association

Printed in China.

Comforting Inspiration
for Women

180
PRAYERS TO
Help You
Sleep

VALORIE QUESENBERRY

BARBOUR
PUBLISHING

INTRODUCTION

Rest is what the physical body needs and craves. It's necessary for optimal body and brain function, emotional well-being, and even increased longevity. But more importantly, rest is needed for our spiritual wholeness. When we don't rest, we're refusing to acknowledge the life principles God put into motion, and we will almost certainly reap the consequences to body, mind, and soul.

Yet, rest is routinely difficult for many of us—and a lack of rest affects almost all of us during some seasons of life. Rest may seem like one of the less important rhythms of life, but it carries many spiritual overtones. When we discipline ourselves to set aside time to rest, we are acknowledging our surrender to God's plan. When we can put ourselves in His hands at night, we are committing our lives to His sovereignty. When we can stop our tasks and leave life until tomorrow, we are showing that we are not focusing on work to the exclusion of enjoying the gifts He has given.

Yes, rest is vital. Rest is legitimate. Rest is God-given.

Pray these prayers to help you rest tonight. . .and many nights to come.

Prayers for Blessing

SLEEP WITHOUT FEAR

*"You must not fear them, for the LORD
your God Himself fights for you."*
DEUTERONOMY 3:22 NKJV

. . . .

Dear Father, thank You for loving me as Your precious daughter. Because Your Word says that I can give my burdens to You, I bring to You all my fears. When I was a little girl, I feared monsters in the dark, shadows lurking in the closet, and funny noises in the night. Now that I'm grown, I'm still sometimes fearful at night; but it's the known rather than the unknown that keeps me staring at the ceiling, unable to fall asleep.

Lord, real life can be more frightening than my imaginations at times. The fears I have for my future, my family, my relationships, and my daily problems threaten to stamp out the hours of rest I need. So, right now, I bring to You all these things that keep me up at night. You have promised to fight my battles for me, and so I ask You to take this battle of fear and win the victory by Your power. I'm not strong enough, but You are. I will roll my fears into that trust.

In Jesus' name, amen.

SLEEP WITHOUT HATE

*"But I say to you who hear: Love your
enemies, do good to those who hate you."*
LUKE 6:27 NKJV

. . . .

Dear Lord, as I try to sleep tonight, my mind is troubled by thoughts of those who seem to be against me. I don't like having enemies, but You know those in my life who don't speak well of me, who don't like my company, who go out of their way to avoid me, and who find fault with all I say and do.

I know Jesus experienced this when He was on earth. There were people out to get Him, to trap Him, to find fault with whatever He said and did. Yet, on the cross He prayed for them, leaving me the example of how I should handle my own enemies.

Tonight, I ask that You would reach out in Your grace to those who wish me ill, Father. Guide them into Your truth, protect their families, and extend Your grace to all of us.

In Christ's name, amen.

SLEEP WITHOUT SHAME

Hide Your face from my sins,
and blot out all my iniquities.
PSALM 51:9 NKJV

. . . .

O God, I come to You tonight with confidence in Your truth and praise for Your power. So many times in my life, before I knew You, I went to bed with feelings of guilt hanging over me like a suffocating pile of blankets. But because Your Spirit has worked in my life, Your grace covers me like a warm quilt. I don't have to fear, I don't have to cower, I don't have to hide from You.

Thank You for taking away my shame by the power that is in Your redeeming blood. Thank You for giving me the joy of forgiveness in exchange for my sins. Thank You for opening up the gifts of Your blessing to me as I acknowledge You in my life. Thank You for giving me the promise that You will be in all of my tomorrows, helping me to be victorious in each one of them.

No one is like You, Lord, and I sleep tonight with joy in belonging.

Amen.

SLEEP WITHOUT ENVY

Be not envious of evil men, nor desire to be with them.
PROVERBS 24:1 AMPC

. . . .

O Lord, when I drive home from work or shopping or errands and pass the nice neighborhoods full of plush homes with sprawling drives, gleaming vehicles, and perfectly manicured lawns, I'm tempted to be envious. When I see the parents whose kids are on traveling teams or attend Ivy League universities or win scholarships for achievement, I'm tempted to be envious. When I look around at the way those who follow the culture around them are accepted and given favor and accolades, I'm tempted to be envious.

But then I remember that those who trust in these things, who place high value on them, are not following the kingdom of heaven. And to prioritize the things of this earth is to be evil. Lord, as I go to sleep tonight, set an envy alarm to go off when I wake if ever I prize anything more than You.

Amen.

SLEEP WITHOUT CHAOS

*For You have been a stronghold for the poor,
a stronghold for the needy in his distress, a shelter
from the storm, a shade from the heat; for the blast of
the ruthless ones is like a rainstorm against a wall.*
ISAIAH 25:4 AMPC

. . . .

Father God, when my life feels chaotic, I can't seem to fall asleep. My mind whirs with all the various appointments and deadlines and events in the near future. My heart feels guilty for not spending as much time with those I love because I'm scattered in so many directions. My thoughts are disjointed, and praying is hard. When I try to read Your Word, my mind catches on a phrase that reminds me of something I have to do and I lose my focus. I fall into bed exhausted every night, knowing that my dreams will echo the hamster wheel of life.

So tonight, Father, I bring all my bits and pieces to You, all the uncollated pages of my life. Will You help me put them in order? Will You give me the wisdom to prioritize and accomplish what I most need to do? And tonight, will You give me sleep without chaos and with rest for my mind?

In Jesus' name, amen.

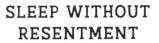

SLEEP WITHOUT RESENTMENT

Let all bitterness and wrath and anger and clamor and
slander be put away from you, along with all malice.
EPHESIANS 4:31 ESV

. . . .

Lord Jesus, You are my perfect example of how to live. When You were reviled and slandered, You did not retaliate; You did not allow a grudge. You loved and forgave.

Tonight, I want to sleep without resentment toward those in my life who have mistreated me. Going to sleep with bitter thoughts is not comforting, despite Satan's lies. Bitterness makes for restless sleep and a troubled mind upon awakening. And most of all, clutching resentment to my heart in the form of painful memories, revolving thoughts of hurts, and daydreams of revenge is a sin. I want to be obedient to Your call to forgiveness.

I ask You, by Your power, to enable me to set my will to forgive and not to hold the debt over the offender's head. You will take care of justice. I would do it wrongly. I will focus on You and Your overcoming grace and go to sleep trusting You to work all things out.

Amen.

SLEEP WITHOUT DISCONTENTMENT

For we brought nothing into this world, and it is certain we can carry nothing out. And having food and clothing, with these we shall be content.
1 Timothy 6:7–8 NKJV

· ·

Dear God, You are the Creator and provider of all things. From You, all things have their beginning—men, women, the animals, the earth, and everything in it. We get wrapped up in our possessions here on earth, forgetting that all of it will be burned up someday and that only eternity really matters and the people who will populate it.

The apostle Timothy, under the inspiration of Your Holy Spirit, reminds us that we come into the world as naked infants. And we leave this world, usually, as old people—wizened and without baggage. Our stuff makes us happy for a little while, but it's not lasting.

Tonight, as I go to sleep, I make the choice to be thankful for the many things I do have. It's hard to remember that the promise of ease and enjoyment that comes with having more stuff is an illusion. Stuff doesn't stay with us, Lord, but You will.

Amen.

SLEEP WITHOUT GUILT

*Eagerly waiting for the revelation of our Lord Jesus
Christ, who will also confirm you to the end, that you
may be blameless in the day of our Lord Jesus Christ.*
1 CORINTHIANS 1:7–8 NKJV

. . . .

Lord, guilt is a gift when we've done something wrong. It's
Your wake-up call, the prod You use to remind us we need
to make things right, the sickening feeling we get when
we've sinned, the disturbance of our peace in the night.

Guilt is a terrible nighttime companion. Humans were
instead made for unbroken fellowship with our Creator.
This is why so many people drink in the night, use illegal
substances, or try to numb their consciences with illicit
romantic affairs. Guilt contributes to mental and emotional
illness and is the unhappy soundtrack of those who sit in
prison.

Lord, thank You for coming to set us free from sin and
the guilt that goes with it. Because of Jesus and His redemptive work in me, I can go to sleep tonight with a clear conscience, blameless before God. This gives me soul rest as
well as body rest. Thank You, Jesus.

Amen.

SLEEP WITHOUT TORMENT

*There is no fear in love; but perfect love casts
out fear, because fear involves torment.*
1 JOHN 4:18 NKJV

. . . .

Lord God, tonight I bring to You my torment. I live in an earthly body, subject to human stimuli, tainted with imperfection, decaying little by little. And I live with an earthly mind that is prone to miscalculation and misinterpretation, to errors in judgment and inaccurate perceptions.

When I focus on my human fallibility, I feel tormented. Though my motive is right, I'm incapable of perfect execution; there will always be rough edges in my life for You to work on. I'm glad You don't count these as sin, but rather view them as a parent would look at a small child who tries his best to do what he is asked but doesn't have the capacity yet to do it well.

You are my Father, and I'm so glad for Your patience as I grow in spiritual understanding. As I release my day and my mind and body into Your hands for safekeeping through the night, I choose to look to Your perfect love that reminds me that You are perfecting me every day that I live and obey.

In Jesus' name, amen.

SLEEP WITHOUT SPITEFULNESS

*Lord, my heart is not haughty, nor my eyes
lofty; neither do I exercise myself in matters too
great or in things too wonderful for me.*
PSALM 131:1 AMPC

. . . .

Dear Father in heaven, when I feel put down or inadequate, I'm tempted to become haughty or spiteful. Satan wants me to preen my feathers and use a sarcastic tone, to imagine that I'm being persecuted and have a right to a disdainful manner. But I know this is not of You. You call me to holiness in my attitude and actions, whether I've been treated well or not.

I don't want to be characterized by spitefulness, Father, so I ask You to be Lord over my emotions and my reactions. When I'm mistreated, cause me to remember Your steadfast grace, which can enable me to respond in a Christ-like manner in any situation.

As I lay my head on my pillow tonight, I rejoice in the knowledge that You have the power to keep me true, no matter what others do. I will make much of Your strength! Amen.

SLEEP WITHOUT FOOD ADDICTION

*So kill (deaden, deprive of power) the evil desire lurking
in your members [those animal impulses and all that
is earthly in you that is employed in sin]: sexual vice,
impurity, sensual appetites, unholy desires, and all
greed and covetousness, for that is idolatry (the deifying
of self and other created things instead of God).*
COLOSSIANS 3:5 AMPC

O God, before I sleep tonight, I bring to You my struggle
with food. I know You created food, and that makes it good.
You created our bodies to be able to process food, and You
created our mouths with taste buds and our noses with the
ability to smell so that we can not only use food for fuel but
also enjoy the taste of it. I don't want to think of food as sin.
It is not evil, no matter what others say. Chocolate cake is
not sinful. I don't need to punish myself for enjoying food.

But, Lord, sometimes I'm tempted to use food in a
wrong way, to turn to it for comfort and to obsess over it
when I feel deprived. And so, Lord, I ask You to help me
surrender my eating habits and use food as an offering of
worship. You've made food to nourish me and never to be
my master. Let me use food and not let it use me.

In Jesus' name, amen.

SLEEP WITHOUT ALARM

He shall cover you with His feathers, and under His wings you shall take refuge; His truth shall be your shield and buckler. You shall not be afraid of the terror by night, nor of the arrow that flies by day.

PSALM 91:4–5 NKJV

. . . .

Dear Lord, as I prepare for sleep tonight, I'm grateful that You watch over me. Nothing is quite as startling as being suddenly awakened in the middle of the night because of a loud noise or a blaring siren or a terrific storm. These things cause me to be alarmed, to be shaken out of a dream world into an unknown event. I'm thankful that You see everything that happens in the night, and You are in control. Nothing comes as a surprise to Your courts.

Lord, *terror* is a good word to describe the feeling of adrenaline and panic that hits when tragedy happens at night or when dangers are at hand. Because You are watching in the night, I can be sure that even if something terrible happens, I won't have to face it alone. And I'm reassured to remember that those who put their trust in You have You as their protector. Most of the time, the terror in our imaginations is the result of a bad dream, so help me not to give undue weight to its fervor.

I lean on You, Lord, as I sleep.

Amen.

SLEEP WITHOUT GLOOMINESS

*I will delight myself in Your statutes; I will
not forget Your word. . . . Your testimonies
also are my delight and my counselors.*
PSALM 119:16, 24 AMPC

. . . .

Dear Father God, sleep can make me gloomy. Things shut down at night—stores close, lights dim, people retire, laughter stops—the cycle of daily life is silenced. When I think about pulling the shades and darkening the house, something inside me feels depressed. It feels as though the world is pulling in on itself. It seems that life is buried in the tomb of sleep. I know this gloominess is illogical, for the very meaning of rest is to stop activity, but it affects me anyway. Perhaps that's why so many deaths occur at night, so many crimes are committed in the night hours, and so much abuse and addiction happen during the night. Humans are susceptible to the downturn of nighttime, and without the grace of Jesus, they may deal with it in sinful ways.

Tonight, Lord, I will focus on Your Word. It shows me how to live, it promises me hope, and it nourishes my soul. Thank you that I can go to sleep without feeling gloomy.

Amen.

SLEEP WITHOUT ANXIETY

*O my God, my life is cast down upon me [and I
find the burden more than I can bear]; therefore
will I [earnestly] remember You from the land of
the Jordan [River] and the [summits of Mount]
Hermon, from the little mountain Mizar.*
PSALM 42:6 AMPC

. . . .

Dear Father, today has been filled with activities, challenges, and yes, stress. As I come to You before I sleep, I know that You've seen all that has gone into my day. You have counted the minutes of my day and offered me grace for every one of them. You have not forsaken me. You are only a breath away from me.

Instead of dwelling on my anxiety tonight over things undone and things done inadequately, I will remember You. I will remember that You are the God who parted the Jordan River and the God who gave the heights of Mount Hermon to Your people. You are the God of little mountains too, like the problems in my life tonight. So I choose to remember You and not dwell on what is past. I look to You, the God of my mountains tomorrow!

Amen.

SLEEP WITHOUT LYING

"Behold, you trust in deceptive words to no avail. Will you steal, murder, commit adultery, swear falsely, make offerings to Baal, and go after other gods that you have not known, and then come and stand before me in this house, which is called by my name, and say, 'We are delivered!'—only to go on doing all these abominations?"
JEREMIAH 7:8–10 ESV

O Lord, I don't want to trust in deceptive words, in my own conception of who You are, in the culture's definition of right and wrong, in the enemy's whispers to me about You. I want to know the truth. This world tells me either that there is no God at all to whom we will answer or that He is all love and no justice, a grandfather type who is easy to manipulate and has no stipulations for sharing His heaven. I know that both of these ideas are untrue.

As Your child, I can't just do whatever I want and then come to You at night and ask You to bless me. As I climb into bed tonight, I pray for Your Holy Spirit to open my eyes to truth in ever-progressing ways. Let me be not deceived but calmed and kept at peace by Your truth.

In Jesus' name, amen.

SLEEP WITHOUT SURLINESS

The foolishness of a man twists his way,
and his heart frets against the LORD.
PROVERBS 19:3 NKJV

. . . .

Father God, I want my heart to be clean and open before You. I don't want to have a nasty, combative, surly spirit. I ask You right now to show me any areas in my life where I'm selfishly choosing my own ways of responding instead of submitting to Your Word.

I put my life in Your hands and my words before Your review. I don't want to go to bed at night and remember reacting to others in ways that displeased You. I pray that You would remind me daily that peace at night is worth the denial of self during the day.

Lord, the Bible is filled with admonitions not to be foolish or angry or undisciplined. You know we need guidelines and boundaries. And what is wonderful is that You give us the strength to honor Your Word when we seek after it.

I place myself in Your providence for the night and under your lordship for tomorrow. Lead me in the way I should go.

In Jesus' name, amen.

SLEEP WITHOUT HARSH WORDS

The words of the wise heard in quiet are better
than the shouting of a ruler among fools.
ECCLESIASTES 9:17 ESV

. . . .

Dear Father God, in my life, I have discovered that words can hurt. And they can heal. As I come to You before I rest for the night, I'm reminded that the words I speak to others matter. They matter because they reveal what's in my heart, and they matter because I'm to steward them well for the good of others and for Your glory. Harsh words hurt. And they linger in the halls of our lives much longer than other things that happen. I don't want to be lulled into believing that my words are my business.

The Bible tells me that my life is open to You. You care about all the things I do with my body, including my speech. I want to be able to drop off to sleep at night with no worries about what I've said. I want to apologize quickly if I offend someone, choose my words carefully when I'm relaxed and chatty, and refuse to gossip or speak in cruel ways to those around me. I ask that You would govern my words tomorrow.

In Jesus' name, amen.

SLEEP WITHOUT PANIC

You will not fear the terror of the night,
nor the arrow that flies by day.
PSALM 91:5 ESV

. . . .

O Lord, thank You that You are the same in the night hours as in the daytime. Night is always worse for us on earth: problems seem bigger, obstacles seem higher, death seems closer, faith seems harder. But these are untruths from the evil one, the father of lies.

These thoughts that come to my mind can cause panic to swell up in my spirit. If I dwell on them, then I start to feel a suffocating terror coming over me. So in the powerful name of Jesus, I resist the temptation to dwell on the wonderings about tomorrow and choose by an act of my will to focus on the mercy and grace and empowerment You can give me to overcome anything for Your glory.

If there is in me anything that would hinder Your work in my life, please show me so that I can surrender it to You. Give me the wisdom I need to make good decisions tomorrow so that I can be victorious in the life You've laid out before me.

I ask these things in the name of Jesus, my Savior. Amen.

SLEEP WITHOUT PAIN

*For my sighing comes instead of my bread, and my
groanings are poured out like water. For the thing that
I fear comes upon me, and what I dread befalls me.*
JOB 3:24–25 ESV

. . . .

Dear Father God, pain is part of this world in which I live. It
is the result of the curse on our earth that won't be erased
until You make all things new. Pain in the night is difficult to
bear. When pain prevents sleep, the night hours are filled
with misery—and the next day is filled with fatigue. There
are times when, like Job, I feel that my groanings pour out
of me as easily as water runs out of an overflowing pot.

I ask tonight that You would give me rest for my body.
If it be in accordance with Your will, please keep back the
pain or give me the knowledge of what medical or naturo-
pathic intervention I should use to keep it at bay. I know
that Your perfect plan for us does not include pain, and I
look forward to that day! In the meantime, thank You for
giving me grace to bear whatever You allow into my life.

In Jesus' name, amen.

SLEEP WITHOUT VANITY

*Pride goes before destruction, and a haughty spirit
before a fall. It is better to be of a lowly spirit with
the poor than to divide the spoil with the proud.*
PROVERBS 16:18–19 ESV

. . . .

Heavenly Father, thank You for the day I've just lived. Thank
You for grace that enabled me to make good choices and
for peace that stayed with me and for hope that helps me
look forward to tomorrow. Thank You for the accomplishments of today. Lord, I ask that You would give me a heart
of wisdom and humility so that I never gloat in my successes
as though they are all of my own doing.

Help me to remember that each breath I take comes
from You, that You keep my heart pumping and my brain
whirring, that You give strength to my hands and feet, and
that without these blessings I would not have been able to
complete my tasks today. My very life is because of You,
and that means everything I do is because of You as well.
I want to go to sleep tonight giving all the glory back to
You—the one to whom it's due.

Amen.

SLEEP WITHOUT GREED

If riches increase, do not set your heart on them. God has spoken once, twice I have heard this: that power belongs to God.
PSALM 62:10–11 NKJV

....

Lord God, it's easy for me to think about the things I want as I prepare for nighttime. The things I don't have rise up before me, calling me to focus on my wants to bring me happiness for tomorrow. But Your Word tells me that riches (or things bought with riches) don't bring joy; they don't have the power to secure my future or make me content. The new outfit or living room set or bigger house or renovated porch or whatever it might be is only something to be enjoyed within the context of Your peace in my life and within the parameters of Your will for me.

The more I have, Lord, the more I will need to manage and store. And storage problems bring stress, not calm. Only You have the power to make my life beautiful. It's fine for me to enjoy nice things and even to buy them within my means. But help me, Father, not to begin to believe that they are the strength behind my serenity. I ask You tonight to help me deliberately deny greed by focusing on You and not stuff.

Amen.

SLEEP WITHOUT
BAD THOUGHTS

*O LORD, You have searched me and known
me. You know my sitting down and my rising
up; You understand my thought afar off.*
PSALM 139:1–2 NKJV

Dear Lord, so often I'm plagued by errant thoughts that
float into my mind. I don't want them, and I don't intend
them, but they come to my consciousness with their filth
and their evil and their temptation. They make me feel
unclean and guilty.

But I'm glad I know that You can discern which thoughts
are really my own and which ones are shot into my brain
from the devil. I know he wants to get me to latch on to
one of those suggestions and act on it. But by the power
of Jesus' blood, I can resist temptation and be victorious.
I don't have to respond to the thought with acceptance.
And it's not sin when I refuse to let it become part of my
plan for the day.

And so I ask You again to be Lord of my mind. Help me
remember Your Word and turn to its truth for empowerment. As I sleep tonight, wash Your promises over my mind,
and let me wake up ready for another day.

Amen.

SLEEP WITHOUT ESTRANGEMENT

"If you meet your enemy's ox or his donkey going astray, you shall surely bring it back to him again. If you see the donkey of one who hates you lying under its burden, and you would refrain from helping it, you shall surely help him with it."
EXODUS 23:4–5 NKJV

. . . .

Father in heaven, it goes against my natural human inclinations to do nice things for those who don't seem to like me or those I don't enjoy being around. Sometimes these people are in my own family. It's difficult to think of them pleasantly.

But I want to go to sleep tonight with a clear conscience and with love in my heart for everyone, just as You command. So I ask You for grace and discernment to act on Your truth tomorrow and do something nice for those from whom I feel estranged. Give me ideas for how to accomplish it without it being awkward or preachy. Help me to serve in an unobtrusive way—not only for the other's benefit but so that I might know the discipline and joy of serving someone else. And I know this will help to change my attitude toward that person too.

In Jesus' name, amen.

SLEEP WITHOUT OBSESSING

Roll your works upon the Lord [commit and trust them wholly to Him; He will cause your thoughts to become agreeable to His will, and] so shall your plans be established and succeed.
PROVERBS 16:3 AMPC

. . . .

Father God, one of my human frailties is my inclination to obsess over things that are ahead of me or behind me, things I can't change. These events and plans and responsibilities weigh on me. These words I have spoken haunt me. These wonderings about others' motives or assessment of me continually trail me. I want to let go, but I feel trapped in a house of mirrors. Everywhere I look, those obsessive thoughts are coming at me from another angle.

The only thing I know to do is to obey Your Word. It tells me to roll my works (past and present) upon You and commit my future works into Your hand. Then You'll help my thoughts about the future to be in agreement with Your will, and You'll establish or make firm the things I will do.

I know it's not Your plan for me to obsess about the future or the past. Please grant me restful sleep tonight so I may enter the new day ahead with hopeful anticipation.

Amen.

SLEEP WITHOUT BITTERNESS

*Does a spring pour forth from the same opening
both fresh and salt water? Can a fig tree,
my brothers, bear olives, or a grapevine produce
figs? Neither can a salt pond yield fresh water.*
JAMES 3:11–12 ESV

O God, I ask for Your grace tonight so that I can be a woman who doesn't allow bitter words to be part of my daily interaction with others. As I speak with my family and my coworkers and my church group and my neighbors, check me when I start to express myself with a wrong attitude, and help me to deal sternly with the selfishness that precedes such an attitude. Anytime I give in to bitterness, I'm affirming that I prefer my own way of dealing with others (resentment) instead of Your way of dealing with them (mercy). I don't want to be like a nonbearing tree or a salty pond. I want to be a tree that blossoms with nourishment and a spring of life-giving words.

Lord, today is past, and tomorrow is waiting. I surrender myself and my words and my attitudes to You anew. Let my speech and my motives issue forth from a spirit of love for others, a spirit that has been made compassionate by Your Holy Spirit.

I ask these things in Jesus' name. Amen.

SLEEP WITHOUT APPREHENSION

*Do not be afraid of sudden terror or of the ruin of
the wicked, when it comes, for the Lord will be your
confidence and will keep your foot from being caught.*
PROVERBS 3:25–26 ESV

Dear Lord, as I try to go to sleep tonight, I'm reaching out
to You with my agitation and angst. I'm having a hard time
letting go of the negative possibilities in my imagination.
I'm struggling with my doubts. I want to have faith. I want
to place my total confidence in You so that I can sleep at
rest in Your plan.

So many sudden things could happen to change my life
in drastic ways. The enemy likes to bring these possibilities to my mind and distract me from Your truth. But I'm
determined to obey Your voice and remember the promises
You've made to watch over me and guide me and keep me.

Right now, I pray that Your hand of grace and wisdom
and protection would be upon my life tomorrow as I wake
and head into a new day. And tonight, trusting You, I will
sleep without the burden of my thoughts.

Amen.

SLEEP WITHOUT BODY HATRED

*But who are you, O man, to answer back to God? Will
what is molded say to its molder, "Why have you made
me like this?" Has the potter no right over the clay?*
ROMANS 9:20–21 ESV

. . . .

Creator God, this is one of my hardest battles.

You made me for beauty. You created me as a woman.
I'm made in Your image in an earthly female modality,
fashioned by Your hand to reflect Your life-giving and nourishing qualities—Your gentle, loyal, and sacrificial love. The
opposites of male and female glorify You in their complete
image of Your likeness.

But much of the time, I don't especially like the body
You gave me. That sounds terrible and ungrateful, but I
confess it's true. The ravages of the curse have left their
mark on my DNA; I inherited some traits that are unlovely.
Aging and gravity are having their way with my face and
form. So many times, I feel ugly and ungraceful.

Tonight, Lord, as I go to sleep, help me to remember
that I am the only one who can glorify You in this body.
And someday, You will make it perfect and new. Remind
me that hating or disliking myself amounts to despising
Your creation, and that's wrong.

Thank You, Father, for loving me as Your precious
daughter. Amen.

SLEEP WITHOUT ANGER

*Be ye angry, and sin not: let not the
sun go down upon your wrath.*
EPHESIANS 4:26 KJV

. . . .

Dear Lord, thank You for redeeming my nature and giving me the ability to refrain from releasing my anger in self-centered and sinful ways. By trusting in Your Holy Spirit and following His leading, I won't let my anger cause me to hurt others.

It's normal to have feelings of irritation and frustration, but it's never right to mistreat others when I'm feeling upset. You gave me the perfect example to follow. When others mocked You and spit on You, You didn't retaliate. When others said bad things about You or doubted who You are, even when they drove nails into Your hands and feet and hung You on a cross, You didn't lash out. Because You won the victory over sin and self, I can be victorious too.

The Bible says I must not let the day slip away while I hold on to my anger. Lord, right now I give my anger to You so that You can help me deal with it appropriately. I know my weakness is no match for Your power. I surrender it to You.

Amen.

SLEEP WITHOUT
NOISY THOUGHTS

*Great peace have they who love Your law; nothing
shall offend them or make them stumble.*
PSALM 119:165 AMPC

. . . .

Dear Lord, my brain is filled with noise tonight. The things
that have challenged me today are still lodged in my thinking. The things I need to do tomorrow are stuck there
too. And besides that, I'm worried about my family and
my other relationships. There are things I can't change in
their lives, but I still feel responsible. At times I feel like my
thoughts drown out the promises of Your Word and the
comfort of Your voice.

So, tonight, I pray that Your Spirit would bring stillness
to my mind. You can quiet the noisy thoughts, just as You
quieted the waves of the sea surrounding a fishing boat
long ago. And when You bring calm, I will be able to listen
to Your truth and act upon it. I ask that You would work
in me so that even my thoughts would reflect the wonder
of Your power.

In Jesus' name, amen.

SLEEP WITHOUT WORRY

*So do not worry or be anxious about tomorrow,
for tomorrow will have worries and anxieties of its
own. Sufficient for each day is its own trouble.*
MATTHEW 6:34 AMPC

. . . .

Heavenly Father, You are the creator, sustainer, and provider of the whole earth. Without You, nothing was made. And nothing will pass away without Your knowledge. This earth will continue for as long as You say.

You know every storm that brews in the heavens and every sunny day that brightens the skies. You know how many animals are nesting or birthing or stalking this very night. You are intimately acquainted with me and my family and our needs.

I'm often tempted to think that the details of my life are unknown to You. I know in my head that You know all things, but in everyday life, it seems fantastic that even the exact number of hairs on my head is firmly established in Your mind. Yet, the Bible tells me this is true. And if that is so, then I can certainly turn to You with my needs for tomorrow.

You already know my needs and how You are planning to meet them. Until then, help me trust. Tomorrow is Yours, Lord.

In Jesus' name, amen.

SLEEP WITHOUT UNFORGIVENESS

But if you do not forgive others their trespasses [their reckless and willful sins, leaving them, letting them go, and giving up resentment], neither will your Father forgive you your trespasses.

MATTHEW 6:15 AMPC

. . . .

Dear Lord, Your Word convicts me with these words. It arrests me in my thinking. The culture around me tells me to get even, to gloat in another's comeuppance, to deny forgiveness to those who wrong me. Those who don't understand forgiveness say that some things cannot be forgiven. But that's not the way Your kingdom works.

You say to forgive anyone and everyone. You will forgive our many sins against You if only we ask. We must do the same for others. We must reflect Your mercy and grace. And if we don't follow You in this, then we're not truly believing and trusting in You and cannot be forgiven ourselves. Having saving faith in You requires that we commit everything to You in that faith—and that means we leave vengeance in Your hands and offer to others what You give to us: forgiveness.

I ask You, Father, as I turn off the light and lie down to rest, to place forgiving grace in my heart to extend to others.

In Jesus' name, amen.

SLEEP WITHOUT REMORSE

*For once you were darkness, but now you are
light in the Lord; walk as children of Light [lead
the lives of those native-born to the Light]. For the
fruit (the effect, the product) of the Light or the
Spirit [consists] in every form of kindly goodness,
uprightness of heart, and trueness of life.*
EPHESIANS 5:8 9 AMPC

. . . .

O Lord, falling asleep is difficult when my thoughts run
to the memories of what I wish I hadn't done. There were
things I did before I knew You as my Savior that rise up
before me like monsters in the dark. There are moments in
my past I would like to forget. There are hurtful things I've
said that I wish could be forever erased from my memory.
There are things for which I've asked Your forgiveness that
continue to haunt me.

I can't undo my sinful past. Yet, You promise in Your
Word that You will make me a new creature, a new being,
through Your redemptive power. That means my past is
forgiven and in Your hands, and it has no power over me
any longer.

I commit my night of rest to You, the God who took my
remorse upon Himself at Calvary and turned my despair
into hope.

In Jesus' name, amen.

SLEEP WITHOUT SELF-LOATHING

I praise you, for I am fearfully and wonderfully made.
Wonderful are your works; my soul knows it very well.
PSALM 139:14 ESV

. . . .

Dear Father God, there is nothing that You do badly. I know that very well. But when it comes to me—my gifts, my personality, my flaws, and my quirks—I don't always act on that knowledge. I'm much harder on myself than I am on my friends. If one of them was feeling stupid for something she said or did, I would remind her that everyone says something silly once in a while; it's human. If she was down on herself because of her personality, I would tell her that variety is good and it's a blessing we're not all alike. If she was saying she didn't have any talents, I would be quick to disagree with her, counting out for her all the things she does well.

Forgive me for focusing on my own perception of my inadequacy. When I'm continually the subject of my own thoughts, there's a problem somewhere. Perhaps a proper view of me comes from a proper view of You that then looks over the horizon to others before it turns to self.

Tonight, Lord, please give me a proper view of You. I turn the eyes of my heart toward You. Amen.

SLEEP WITHOUT DESPAIR

For You are my hope, O Lord GOD;
You are my trust from my youth.
PSALM 71:5 NKJV

. . . .

Lord God, when night falls, it's easy to fall into a melancholy feeling. I think of my life and my struggles, my challenges and my problems. I think of the unfulfilled places in my life, the yearnings for love and cherishing, the wish to be known fully and deeply and yet loved. As twilight turns to night, my soul reaches out for some indefinable something, a fleeting desire for something more than I have known here on earth.

I know, Lord, that only You can satisfy the craving for wholeness that manifests itself in this way. And so I ask that You would help me to choose to dwell in Your love, to deliberately turn my heart to You. You have been the source of my hope since I was a child; You will be my source of hope now.

On this earth, nothing is perfect. But You created our world. You came from heaven to live among us, and You love us perfectly. Drown my despair in Your love. Fill me with hope in You. You will fulfill me, sustain me, and preserve me.

I trust in You, Lord. Amen.

SLEEP WITHOUT HOSTILITY

It is better to dwell in the corner of the housetop
than to share a house with a disagreeing,
quarrelsome, and scolding woman.
PROVERBS 25:24 AMPC

. . . .

Dear Father, as I get ready to slip into bed tonight, I want to ask You to give me a heart that recoils from dissension and strife. Let me not be a woman who finds pleasure in starting squabbles. Sometimes it's necessary to disagree, but I never want to be someone who delights in arguing with others. I don't want to be a quarrelsome woman.

Instead, I want to be a woman who celebrates harmony, who refuses to live in hostility. No house is big enough for a clamorous, disagreeable, grudge-holding person; the cantankerous character of that person takes up too much space.

Please enable me, by Your grace, to live tomorrow with a sweet attitude and a teachable spirit. I want to reflect You in all I do. And help me sleep tonight with no feelings of hostility toward anyone.

In Jesus' name, amen.

SLEEP WITHOUT DREAD

*But whoso hearkens to me [Wisdom] shall
dwell securely and in confident trust and shall
be quiet, without fear or dread of evil.*
PROVERBS 1:33 AMPC

. . . .

O Lord, I want to be able to sleep calmly and confidently.
I want to rest in the knowledge that You hold the edges of
my life, that You see what is coming, that You always go
before me if I put my life in Your hands.

Too many nights I've gone to bed with dread in my
heart—dread to wake up to more stress, dread to carry
on the routines of life, dread to face my confusion and
heartaches—inky, black dread.

But, tonight, I choose to turn my heart to Your wisdom
before I drift off to sleep. I can bolster my courage for the
adventure of tomorrow by surrendering myself anew to
Your divine sovereignty. I can turn over in my bed and close
my eyes, secure in the fact that everything about tomorrow
must wait for Your assent. Thank You that I can trust You
to turn everything for my good and Your glory.

Amen.

Prayers for Relaxation

THE WATER MAKER

But let justice run down like waters and righteousness
as a mighty and ever-flowing stream.
AMOS 5:24 AMPC

. . . .

O Father, tonight as I prepare for bed, I can hear the sound of the water outside. Its spraying, lapping, cascading sound soothes me and makes me want to relax. Yet, the sound of a torrent of water reminds us of the great power water can hold. You created the natural world and all that is in it. You made us to need water in our bodies for life and water in the land for growing things. Without water, there is no life.

Likewise, I'm reminded that righteousness is necessary for spiritual life. There can be only death when one's works are evil. Help me, Lord, to remember that just as the sound of water brings comfort to me, my righteousness through You can bring comfort to another and can give them the drink they need to get back on the path of life.

I will close my eyes as I sleep beside the water and praise You that You bring life to me!

Amen.

THE GLORY OF
THE WOODLANDS

*For every beast of the forest is Mine, and the cattle
on a thousand hills. I know all the birds of the
mountains, and the wild beasts of the field are Mine.*
PSALM 50:10–11 NKJV

. . . .

Creator God, You designed a beautiful world! To You
belongs the glory of the woods and the creatures in them.
By Your design, the trees grow tall from sprouts and their
branches reach toward the heavens. The pine trees release
their spiny cones, and the oak trees offer their acorns. The
silver maple and birch trees wave their shimmering leaves
in the wind. The needles of the fir trees spread the spice
of their aroma all around.

The forest creatures dart to and fro, and the owl sits
nobly on his limb. The deer stops briefly from grazing
and cocks his ear. The birds rest in their lofty homes and
wait for dawn.

I will go to sleep tonight remembering that You alone
sustain the woodlands and their hosts, and that You sustain
me when I trust in You. Amen.

THE SNOWY VAULT

Have you entered the treasuries of the snow,
or have you seen the treasuries of the hail?
JOB 38:22 AMPC

. . . .

Father, sometimes when I'm sleeping, You open the store-houses of heaven and let snow sift down upon the earth. As the moon sends its misty beams downward, the frozen countryside gleams with its soft covering. The creatures run into their burrows, and the temperature plummets in the frosty air. I wake up to a world adrift in snow, to the dead brown of earth transformed by Your gift of white.

Thank You, Lord, for controlling the snow and the changing landscape. I remember that winter is the season of deadness and dormancy. Many people dislike winter. But You have a purpose for it, and You won't let it go unsung and unadorned. You give winter the unique beauty of icicles and encrusted tree branches and a million diamonds glittering on every snow-laden field. In Your treasury of snow, You guard wondrous wealth. And every once in a while, You allow the earth dwellers to see a glimpse of what You own.

I will sleep tonight assured that the one who designs each snowflake has designed my night and my day too.

I love You, Lord. Amen.

THE STORM ACCOUNTANT

The LORD has His way in the whirlwind and in the
storm, and the clouds are the dust of His feet.
NAHUM 1:3 NKJV

. . . .

Jehovah God, storms are often frightening to me. They appear to be uncontrolled, savage, wild. But Your Word tells me that nothing is outside the realm of Your control. I'm glad for that. It means that no matter the fury of the winds or the pelting of the rains, Your purpose and plan will go on.

Like a CPA whose job it is to oversee the income and expenditures for an organization, You look down from heaven and calculate the budget of Your kingdom. And it always reads "no deficit." Your goodness abounds forever; Your providence never runs out. Storms certainly cannot deplete that account.

Sleeping in a storm can be frightening. But sleeping in the care of the Storm Accountant is perfectly assuring. You are the one who calms my storms even while I sleep and wakes me up to another day of Your grace.

Thank You, Lord. Amen.

SUN-MAKER GOD

*Of the heavens has God made a tent for the
sun, which is as a bridegroom coming out of
his chamber; and it rejoices as a strong man to
run his course. Its going forth is from the end of
the heavens, and its circuit to the ends of it; and
nothing[yes, no one] is hidden from the heat of it.*
PSALM 19:4–6 AMP

. . . .

Creator Lord, I'm so thankful You made the sun. Its rays
warm the earth and help things grow. Its cycle is tied to
the seasons just as You ordained. Its brightness brings
encouragement and health to human beings. Throughout
history, pagan mankind has worshipped the sun instead of
its Creator, misplacing the awe and gratitude due to You.
But that orb in the sky could never love us or redeem us; it
is a created thing. You are the one who makes everything
that is beautiful. You make everything that promotes life
and health.

As I lie down in sleep tonight, I look forward to the
rising of the sun tomorrow. Nothing man-made can pre-
vent the dawn; You own it. And I know that when I rise to
meet the challenges and joys and sorrows of a new day, the
Creator of the sun will walk with me if I keep in step with
His purpose for me.

Amen.

MISTS AND SUNRISES

The Lord by wisdom founded the earth; by understanding
He established the heavens; by His knowledge the depths
were broken up, and clouds drop down the dew.
PROVERBS 3:19–20 NKJV

. . . .

Lord Almighty, when I think of various places on earth I imagine a mist rising over the mountains or a steamy dew that evaporates with the morning sun. To me, these images speak of the promise of morning where I would want to sip my hearty cup of coffee and revel in the wonder of another day to live.

You are the God who makes mornings segue into afternoons and evenings. You call us to honor You in our morning routine so that our days will be loaded with the benefits of spending time with You. As the clouds drop the dew in the predawn while night birds find their perch and the rooster practices his strident anthem, I will start my day with the knowledge that all the things of heaven and earth are held safely in Your hand.

But right now, it's night and time for sleep. Into Your keeping I place my life until the sun rises again.

Thank you, Lord God. Amen.

A GUIDE FOR TOMORROW

The LORD God is my strength; He will make my feet like deer's feet, and He will make me walk on my high hills.
HABAKKUK 3:19 NKJV

. . . .

Lord Elohim, praise to You from every peak of earth! You alone made the mountains rise up from nothing. You created the rises and dips and craggy points. You caused the cliffs to appear and the hazy heights to take shape. You are the God of the mountain, the God who walks above the clouds, the God who causes me to triumph.

Because of You, I can rest tonight, confident that You will guide my steps tomorrow on the slippery slopes. You will assuredly guide my footholds as I scale the challenges of family and work and ministry. You will reach out Your hand to me when I come to the place where the path is narrow and the drop-offs are steep. All of this You will do if I ask and surrender my day to You.

Thank You, Lord, for Your excellent care of me. I ask You to be the Shepherd of my tomorrow.

In Jesus' name, amen.

THE ONE WHO MAKES THE RAIN

When He utters His voice—there is a multitude of waters in the heavens: "He causes the vapors to ascend from the ends of the earth; He makes lightnings for the rain; He brings the wind out of His treasuries."

JEREMIAH 51:16 NKJV

. . . .

Jehovah God, rain is not merely the result of meteorological combinations of heat and chill, pressure and wind; rain is the deed You accomplish on the earth by Your decree. You have set weather patterns into place, but none of them can operate without Your call. I don't know how You are involved in the daily schedule of earthly seasons, but I know You are.

Some people like to sleep during a rainstorm, listening to the rhythmic tapping of the droplets on the roof. Some like to wake up to a rainy day, skittering around puddles and watching the world through a misty curtain.

If it's raining tomorrow when I awake, I will know that it's Your doing, what You have ordained. It may not fit my plans, but Your big purpose is more important than my calendar. Tonight, I rest in the knowledge that nothing can happen around me that You won't use for good.

Amen.

A VALLEY PREPARED
FOR NOURISHMENT

*He sends the springs into the valleys; they flow among
the hills. They give drink to every beast of the field;
the wild donkeys quench their thirst. By them the birds of
the heavens have their home; they sing among the branches.*
PSALM 104:10–12 NKJV

. . . .

Heavenly Father, the valleys on earth and in life are often
scorned; they are thought of as places of discouragement
and testing. And perhaps, at times, they are.

But Your Word says that valleys can be nourishing
settings, places where the life-giving springs flow, where
the animals quench their thirst, and where the birds of
the heavens sing. This is the kind of valley You sometimes
give me. These are the seasons when I'm not accomplishing great things or doing anything especially important,
and yet, I'm being the person You created me to be and
enjoying the everyday gifts You give.

I want to be a person who leads others to life-
giving valleys. I want others to look at my life and see the
source of my strength and follow me as I follow You. You
are the one who prepares for us a lush and vibrant valley
where we are refreshed once again.

Amen.

YOU HOLD TOMORROW

*They confronted me in the day of my calamity, but the
LORD was my support. He brought me out into a broad
place; he rescued me, because he delighted in me.*
PSALM 18:18–19 ESV

Sovereign God, calamities and disasters are an unwelcome
part of life on earth. Since sin has entered our world and
cursed everything in it with death, bad things happen. The
natural world is twisted, the biological world is warped,
human beings and animal-kind are afflicted. All of us are
subject to the aberrant and horrific happenings that bring
us sorrow, pain, and loss.

As I get ready to close my eyes in sleep tonight, I'm
aware that nothing I can do will stop bad things from happening. And I know that bad things will continue to occur
until You make all things new. But I also know that You
reign supreme over every event, and—by Your power—You
can redeem the bad and sustain us through every fiery trial.

I don't know what tomorrow holds, O Lord, but I do
know that You hold tomorrow in Your mighty hands and
will help me bear whatever comes my way. Thank You that
I can go to sleep in the calm assurance that I am not alone.

I love You, Father. Amen.

OF COMMUNITY AND REST

*Sing aloud to God our strength; shout for joy to the
God of Jacob! Raise a song; sound the tambourine,
the sweet lyre with the harp. Blow the trumpet at the
new moon, at the full moon, on our feast day.*
PSALM 81:1–3 ESV

· ·

Dear Lord, I love a good celebration, and holidays with the
family I love are the best! Human beings are social beings;
we were made to live in community with others. The first
thing that wasn't good on this earth was for the first man to
be alone. And so You created a suitable mate for him. And
ever since, people have been gathering together to experience life, to celebrate their joys and mourn their griefs.

When I'm gathered with a lot of people, I find it hard
to rest. So much activity is going on, my mind has trouble
calming down enough for me to fall asleep. I know You
understand what I mean, because often the places You
went on this earth were crowded with people. People
wanted to be near You; people wanted to hear You and
get close to You.

Tonight, as I try to get comfortable and relaxed enough
to rest, I ask You to help me reflect You in my interactions
with others. May tomorrow be blessed with Your good and
gracious presence.

Amen.

PRAISES WITHOUT WORDS

O Lord, our Lord, how excellent (majestic and
glorious) is Your name in all the earth! You have
set Your glory on [or above] the heavens. Out of
the mouths of babes and unweaned infants You
have established strength because of Your foes,
that You might silence the enemy and the avenger.
PSALM 8:1–2 AMPC

. . . .

O Father, newborn babies cannot praise You with words, but they praise You with their newborn-ness. As infants, they are garnering exclamations of glory for You. As friends, relatives, and sometimes perfect strangers comment on the beauty and innocence of a new baby, those words are very realistically tributes of praise to the maker of babies.

Babies praise You by eating and cooing and even crying. Crying is a sign of normalcy, a realization that something is wrong. The desire to eat is built into a newborn, and that also honors You. Furthermore, infants can bring You glory by sleeping in sweet, unaffected, restful slumber.

Right now as I'm trying to fall into sleep, I ask You to calm my mind and emotions and give me the sleep of an infant. And in the morning, let me waken with a song of praise on my lips, Lord.

Amen.

THE GOD OF MY REST

*Also, every man to whom God has given riches
and possessions, and the power to enjoy them
and to accept his appointed lot and to rejoice
in his toil—this is the gift of God [to him].*
ECCLESIASTES 5:19 AMPC

. . . .

Dear Father in heaven, I think many of us dream of living in a grand house with a huge master bedroom and plush throws and coverlets. When I walk into the home-goods stores and look at all the luxurious items, I imagine what it would be like to furnish my space with beautiful things. I want to be content with what You've given me, but I also have a love of beauty and refinement that causes me to appreciate lovely items.

Someday, You may give me a different budget and different opportunities than what You've given me today. If that time comes, I will rejoice with every velvet tassel and each inch of fine linen.

But for now, You have given me the gift of rest in my cotton pajamas and passed-down quilt. I will sleep as soundly tonight as I would in a queen's boudoir because You are the God of my rest.

Thank You, Lord. Amen.

PUSHED TOWARD MATURITY

But I have calmed and quieted my soul,
like a weaned child with its mother;
like a weaned child is my soul within me.
PSALM 131:2 ESV

. . . .

God of all, there are times when I protest against what You've seen fit to remove from me. Like a child who is being weaned, I can't understand why my source of happiness and comfort is being removed. I want the familiar, the crutch, the pacifier of my angst.

But You, in Your wisdom, know it's best for me to grow up and learn to adapt without my earthly support system. Like a mother who knows her child must learn to drink from a cup, You withhold baby comforts and push me toward mature life in You.

Tonight, I'm dealing with some tough maturing. I see the ways You are gently prodding me into spiritual maturity. I surrender my all into Your keeping, knowing that even when I can't understand why You allow certain trials, I can trust Your judgment. You know all things.

Help me sleep peacefully tonight, quieted and calmed. In Jesus' name, amen.

REST IN ANY CIRCUMSTANCE

I know how to be brought low, and I know how to abound.
In any and every circumstance, I have learned the secret
of facing plenty and hunger, abundance and need.
I can do all things through him who strengthens me.
PHILIPPIANS 4:12–13 ESV

Jehovah Lord, I have often thought of those in other lands who make their beds on the ground of huts or in a jail cell or in a crowded, communal room. Many around the world don't know the luxury of a bed frame and mattress, sheets and blankets, and a pillow to cradle their head as they rest. I am so blessed in so many ways. I thank You for my many blessings; each one is a gift from You.

If the time comes when You ordain that my daily allowance will be less comfortable than it is now, I trust You to help me learn to live and work and rest in that setting. Please give me a heart of compassion for those who sleep in want tonight—some under bridges and some in city doorways, some in a car packed with all their belongings and some on a park bench. I don't know their stories, but help me to love them as You do.

Give me rest tonight so that I can share Your love tomorrow.

In Jesus' name, amen.

SLEEP IN THE MASTER'S HOUSEHOLD

"Happy are these your servants, who continually stand before you and hear your wisdom!"
2 CHRONICLES 9:7 ESV

. . . .

O God, a lot is said these days about being sons and daughters and children and friends, but I don't hear as much about the fact that we are also your servants. We are adopted into Your family if we have surrendered our lives to You in faith, but there is still the fact that You are the Creator and Master and we are not. I don't want to lose the awareness that You rule over it all and that I am part of that which You are over.

It's easy for human beings to feel entitled, even those who know the truth of Your Word. But we must never lose sight of the fact that we are to be as humble as Jesus was when He walked the earth.

As I lie down to sleep tonight, there are things in my life and surroundings and setting that I wish were different. But because I am your servant and You are the Lord, I will rest in the knowledge that You are guiding the household and that You will not forget Your servant. I trust You.

Amen.

REST FOR THE BATTLE-WEARY

Take [with me] your share of the hardships and suffering [which you are called to endure] as a good (first-class) soldier of Christ Jesus.
2 TIMOTHY 2:3 AMPC

. . . .

Lord and Master, the history books tell of the hardships suffered by soldiers. Those under orders go where the conflict is and sleep when they can. They eat little, walk much, and carry on. Rest is the reward for which they fight—rest for their country, rest for their people, rest for their comrades, and rest for themselves.

In the battle fray, there is little time for sleep. They continue on, advancing ever onward, sacrificing their comfort, their serenity, and perhaps their lives. But they are called to endure. And so am I.

As one who is in the conflict for right—for the kingdom of Christ—I'm called by You to endure temptations and trials and persecutions and sacrifices. But the reward laid before me is rest, eternal rest that does not end.

As I drift off to sleep tonight, help me remember that I am a soldier engaged in war but commissioned for battle by the King of kings.

Amen.

WHERE THE SHEPHERD LEADS

*O come, let us worship and bow down: let us kneel
before the LORD our maker. For he is our God; and we
are the people of his pasture, and the sheep of his hand.*
PSALM 95:6–7 KJV

. . . .

Lord, my Shepherd, I'm glad You are the one who watches
over me. Like a strong and gentle shepherd, You protect me
and care for me and keep Your eyes on me. Nothing enters
the pasture of my life that You cannot see, that You cannot
change, that You cannot redeem for good.

The Bible tells me that sometimes You lead me by shady
pools and sometimes through lush grass, but other times
You take me on paths through fearsome trials and across
barren lands. Yet, even in the chasms of the earth where
death lurks, You are always near. When I'm tired, You
give me rest if I will follow Your direction. Thank You for
knowing what is good for me always.

As night falls, I'm reminded of how much I need a
Shepherd. Your voice to give me direction is the guidance
I crave. Please lead me in Your paths tomorrow, Lord.

In Jesus' name, amen.

LIFE ETERNAL

*For, lo, the winter is past, the rain is over
and gone; the flowers appear on the earth;
the time of the singing of birds is come.*
SONG OF SOLOMON 2:11–12 KJV

. . . .

Sustainer God, when I think of spring, I remember that You are the giver of life. You cause the seeds in the ground to germinate, thrusting the power of life through the dormant shell, bursting through the sod with tenacity and beauty. Spring is the season when all nature comes out of hibernation, frolicking in the delight of sunshine and blossoms and color.

Yes, there are allergies and spring storms and mud and chilly days, but all these are working together to bring forth a change in the season; they are the birth pangs of the weather transition. I see Your hand at work in all the beauty and glory of green and growing things. And I feel rested in my soul knowing that life will go on, that You have ordained the cycle of the seasons and nothing can stop it.

Preparing for sleep tonight, I'm reminded that nothing can thwart the life that is given by You. And that includes my life—both here on earth and for eternity if I trust in You as Savior.

Thank You, Lord God, for the gift of life eternal. Amen.

SUMMER MEMORIES
OF PERFECTION

Thou hast set all the borders of the earth:
thou hast made summer and winter.
PSALM 74:17 KJV

....

Lord Jehovah, if there was a season in the garden of Eden, it was probably like summer—long, warm evenings and bright, sunny days. But I'm sure it was never too hot. Today, our weather patterns are twisted by the curse. But back then, everything was just right.

When I think of summer, I think of relaxation and family gatherings, good food from the garden and evenings on the porch. I remember that everything You make is perfect and complete. It was never Your intent that Your creation would suffer severe cold or heat; these extremes came because of sin in our world. But even though man and woman rebelled and sin entered, You chose to redeem the loss by giving beauty to the diverse seasons.

Still, when I encounter a summer evening, it turns my thoughts toward You and the perfection I will experience in heaven someday. Until then, I will be thankful for every soft night and every sparkling day.

Amen.

A HARVEST OF JOY

You [O Lord] have multiplied the nation and increased their joy; they rejoice before You like the joy in harvest, as men rejoice when they divide the spoil [of battle].
ISAIAH 9:3 AMPC

He who goes out weeping, bearing the seed for sowing, shall come home with shouts of joy, bringing his sheaves with him.
PSALM 126:6 ESV

. . . .

God Almighty, harvesttime is more than a season; it's a mood of celebration, of triumph and security and plenty. When I think of harvest, I have thoughts of pumpkins and apples and hay bales, of spicy-smelling baked goods and glowing hearths. Of the pleasures of home and land.

Many people say that fall is their favorite season, and I think I understand why. The colors are more vibrant in the fall than at any other time. The scents are warm and fragrant, and the sounds of honking geese and crunching leaves and simmering soup are nourishing to the ears and the spirit.

Harvest is, furthermore, a spiritual principle. When we sow the seeds of putting Christ first and loving others and caring for our families and sacrificing for our church and worshipping with our whole hearts, we will reap the harvest of joy and delight.

When I lie down tonight, Lord, remind me to rise tomorrow determined to sow in the Spirit.

Amen.

THE FEASTING LIFE

*All the days of the afflicted are evil, but the
cheerful of heart has a continual feast.*
PROVERBS 15:15 ESV

. . . .

Dear Lord, gathering with family and friends is one of my favorite things to do. And no time is more appropriate for that than holidays, and especially the Christmas season. As the temperatures turn chilly, we swathe our homes in festive garlands and lights, bake delicious goodies, buy gifts to show our love, and spend time together. The glory of the season is the birth of Your Son. And around that sacred center spreads an ever-widening circle of feasting and worshipping and gathering.

The Bible tells me that when I have a cheerful heart, I can have the feeling of Christmas all year long. That's what I want to have. Every day of the year, I want to hold in my inner being the quiet celebration of joy that spills out to others and makes every day better because You're in it.

Tonight, as I slip beneath my blankets, I remember the thrill of Christmastime. And I determine in my heart to be one of those who experiences a continual feast because of You, Lord.

Amen.

AN AMBASSADOR TOMORROW

Therefore, we are ambassadors for Christ,
God making his appeal through us.
2 CORINTHIANS 5:20 ESV

Lord Jesus, since I've believed in You for salvation, I thank You for calling me one of Your ambassadors. Serving Your kingdom is the highest honor! I know You've commissioned me to reflect Your love and carry Your light to a needy world. As I follow You every day, You show me opportunities to share Your message of redemption with those around me. Nothing is more important to me than living the life to which You've called me.

Tonight, I go to sleep knowing that I have the best job in the whole world. While I may perform ordinary tasks tomorrow, I know I'm doing them out of my love for You. Whether I'm providing care, working, serving, cleaning, driving, worshipping, shopping, or running errands, I am actually being an ambassador, representing my Savior and Lord.

Please give me strength to shine for You tomorrow, Lord. Amen.

KEPT LIKE A PRINCESS

According to his great mercy, he has caused us to be born again to a living hope through the resurrection of Jesus Christ from the dead, to an inheritance that is imperishable, undefiled, and unfading, kept in heaven for you, who by God's power are being guarded through faith for a salvation ready to be revealed in the last time.

1 Peter 1:3–5 esv

. . . .

O Lord, thank You for Your great love toward me.

As a little girl, I read stories of a beautiful princess who was taken captive by someone evil and then rescued by a brave prince. My little-girl heart wanted to be part of something like that. Yet, as I grew, I realized that fairy tales don't happen in real life, and I gave up on my daydream.

But when I found You as my Savior, I found a love that restored me, a love that cherishes me and keeps me. Like a princess in a castle protected by her warrior, I am kept safe by You. I don't have to fear the onslaught of the enemy against the walls of my soul. In You, I am secure.

As I lie down to sleep in my ordinary bed, inside I know that I am living in a royal chamber because I belong to You.

Thank You, Jesus. Amen.

BETTER THAN A BODYGUARD

*"Come out from among them and be separate, says
the Lord. Do not touch what is unclean, and I will
receive you. I will be a Father to you, and you shall be
My sons and daughters, says the LORD Almighty."*
2 CORINTHIANS 6:17–18 NKJV

....

Holy Father, in You there is forgiveness and cleansing and restoration. Because of Your death on Calvary, I have a place in Your family. Because You cared for me even at my worst, I can have a life with You for the best. I'm blessed to live in relationship with You.

Earthly mothers and fathers do their best to raise their children in good ways. But You always do what is right. You're the one who models what fatherhood should be in myriad ways. Now that I know You, I can rest in the fact that You are guiding me always and loving me continually.

Sleep tonight will come easier when I keep close to my heart the fact that I am Your beloved daughter, and nothing can get by Your watch over me. I don't need a human bodyguard, because I have You.

Amen.

SLEEP WELL, LIKE AN HEIR

The Spirit Himself bears witness with our spirit that we
are children of God, and if children, then heirs—heirs
of God and joint heirs with Christ, if indeed we suffer
with Him, that we may also be glorified together.
ROMANS 8:16–17 NKJV

. . . .

Father God, You have called me and redeemed me and
made me part of Your family. Because I have been born
again through faith in Your Son, I am now a joint heir with
Christ. What an amazing thought! Whether I ever have an
inheritance here on earth from a relative who passes away,
I am assured of an inheritance in heaven. Thank You for
paying the price for my sin with Your own blood.

If I inherited great wealth from a relative, I might sleep
a bit more securely. I would know that my future was taken
care of and that, no matter the emergency, I would have
the funds to find a solution. How much more should I
sleep well because I'm a heavenly heir? All of heaven is at
Your disposal, and You share all Your riches with me. I will
turn off my light and go to sleep in confidence.

Amen.

Prayers for Rest

GOOD DAYS AND SLEEP

*Every good gift and every perfect gift is from above,
and comes down from the Father of lights, with
whom there is no variation or shadow of turning.*
JAMES 1:17 NKJV

. . . .

Father God, all good things come from You, even the gift
of sleep. *Especially* the gift of sleep. Thank You, Lord, for
making our bodies with the ability to rest. And thank You
for the good days I experience when things seem right in
my world and sleep comes easily. That doesn't happen all
the time. There are days when it seems my world is upside
down and I lie awake for a long time trying to turn off my
thoughts.

But tonight as I pull back the sheets and set my alarm,
I'm grateful for the reprieve from trials that You give and for
the hope I have in You that my future is going to be okay. As
the stars twinkle outside and the nocturnal animals rouse
themselves and the earth prepares for quiet, I'm confident
You will watch over me until tomorrow.

I love You, Lord. Amen.

REST WHEN THINGS ARE WRONG

For in the time of trouble He shall hide me in His
pavilion; in the secret place of His tabernacle He
shall hide me; He shall set me high upon a rock.
PSALM 27:5 NKJV

Heavenly Father, days of trouble come to me sometimes. Life is not perfect or easy. I've lived long enough to know that things go wrong and people get sick and cars break down and bills come due and friends move and loved ones die.

Bad things happen, not because You want them to, but because they are the result of the decay in our world. Trials are a reminder that we were made for another world— and that we can go there to be with You if we put our faith in Christ.

While hard days are difficult to experience, the nights that follow can be difficult too. Trying to sleep after receiving bad news can be a challenge. I'm glad I have You to talk to even in the middle of the night. I can turn to You at any time.

This night, while I complete my nightly routine, I choose to focus my thoughts on You and remember that no matter how hard the days get, I am never alone.

Thank You, Lord. Amen.

TESTING TIMES AND SLEEP

"Behold, I have refined you, but not as silver;
I have tested you in the furnace of affliction."
ISAIAH 48:10 NKJV

. . . .

Almighty Father, when times of testing come, sleep is far from me. I can toss and turn on my bed for hours, not getting any rest and sabotaging my day tomorrow. Yet, I know the Bible mentions many people who experienced days of testing.

The one who usually comes to mind is Job, the man who endured more than most of us can imagine. He lost his farm, his home, and his children in one day. And his wife became bitter instead of supporting him. This was severe testing. And yet he maintained his steadfast hope in the Lord. I wonder how he slept at night? I'm sure he was miserable with the boils on his body and the ashes of his house around him. Even so, he remained faithful in the furnace.

Lord, as I end this day, I don't know when my next season of testing will come. But when it does, I want to be equipped with a faith in You that will withstand the melting heat of the fire. When I wake up in the morning, remind me, Lord, that putting You first will result in victory.

Amen.

SLEEP IS A REWARD

*Be strong, therefore, and let not your hands be weak
and slack, for your work shall be rewarded.*
2 CHRONICLES 15:7 AMPC

. . . .

Lord God, there is an old sentiment that one sleeps well
after working hard. I think it's true. When we expend our
energy in manual labor, we rest better at night. Our muscles
finally relax, our brains slip into drowsiness, our nerves
unwind, and our body is rejuvenated.

Rest after hard work is rewarding. When we are profit-
able and contributing and able to perform, we feel gratified
when we do the last task and then go to bed. This is something You built into the human psyche. And it still works!

As I contemplate my work tomorrow, remind me that
sleep is a reward for staying on task and giving the task my
best. And in so doing, I bring honor to You!

Amen.

WORKDAYS ARE IMPORTANT

For even when we were with you, we commanded you
this: If anyone will not work, neither shall he eat.
2 Thessalonians 3:10 nkjv

. . . .

Holy God, I want to walk in the ways You have laid out for living. One of those is that we should work with our hands to provide what we need. None of us should be dependent on others if we have the ability to work and earn money. This is a principle that failed kingdoms and nations have learned to their detriment.

As this day cones to a close, I want to thank You for providing a task and a purpose for me. Help me never to abuse the trust You've given to me. I can get up tomorrow morning and know that You are already there wherever I find myself and in whatever job-related position I have to fill. Thank You for helping me work within my home and in ministry to others as You lead.

I love You, Lord, and I say good night to You now. Thank You for watching over me so well.

Amen.

THE LORD'S DAY

"For in six days the Lord made the heavens
and the earth, the sea, and all that is in them,
and rested the seventh day. Therefore the Lord
blessed the Sabbath day and hallowed it."
EXODUS 20:11 NKJV

. . . .

O God, thank You for making this day of rest in the week. If You hadn't mandated it, I probably wouldn't honor it—and You knew that. So, You put into our world this principle of rest—one day in seven. I want to honor it as I honor You.

When I think about rest and sleep on a daily basis, I remember that You built sleep into our bodily needs. And then You created one whole day dedicated to rest and worship. It's a hallowed thing to rest.

I come to You before I go to sleep tonight and ask that You would be Lord over my week and over my day of rest. I put my full confidence in You to take care of all the little details and give me the assurance I need that You have everything well in hand, and all I need to do is follow Your plan.

Thank You, Father. Amen.

SLEEP WHEN YOU'RE YOUNG

*Remember [earnestly] also your Creator [that you
are not your own, but His property now] in the
days of your youth, before the evil days come or
the years draw near when you will say [of physical
pleasures], I have no enjoyment in them.*
ECCLESIASTES 12:1 AMPC

. . . .

Lord God, You tell me in Your Word that this life is not
forever. We will all stand before You someday to give
account of the things done in the body. You want me to lay
up treasure in heaven and not focus on things on the earth.

The wise writer of Ecclesiastes was inspired to remind
us that some things are easy when you're young but difficult
when you're aged. He called them the "evil days." They
are evil, in that old age robs us of our dignity and inde-
pendence; they can return us to a childish state. And older
people often struggle to get restful and restorative sleep.

You want us to care for our bodies and establish good
patterns when we're young so that when we grow old, we
won't suffer the ill effects of addictions and eating disorders and careless diets.

Help me tomorrow as I wake to commit to caring for
this body so that rest will never be taken from me as a
consequence for sin.

Amen.

SLEEP WHEN YOU'RE OLD

The silver-haired head is a crown of glory,
if it is found in the way of righteousness.
PROVERBS 16:31 NKJV

. . . .

God Almighty, You are the God of every season. I want to honor You with the changing years of my life. As I grow older each year, I know I will face new challenges and new temptations.

There are good things about growing older, but being able to sleep well is not one of them. When my body creaks and groans and protests, I know I'm closer to heaven than I was before. Yet, You have a purpose for me that I still need to fulfill.

Your Word tells me that silvery hair is a crown. I don't believe kings and queens wear their crowns to bed, but the natural one You give us is one we take with us everywhere. It shows to others that we are part of those who have loved You long and followed You to the end. Whether I sleep well or not in the coming years, help me never to forget who I am in Christ.

Amen.

TAKING CARE OF HOME

*So we are always confident, knowing that while we
are at home in the body we are absent from the Lord.*
2 CORINTHIANS 5:6 NKJV

. . . .

Dear Lord Jesus, home is the place where we abide. It's the dwelling where we relax and nourish ourselves and rest. It's a place we share with others. It's our base, the hub of our lives. This is what You gave us when You established the family.

This verse speaks to me deeply when it reminds me that being home in my body is where I reside now, and maintaining that home is important. I need to eat right, get sleep, and bathe and dress and get exercise. This is how I care for the bodily home You've given me.

But someday, when You say it's time, I will go to Your home. I will leave this body here on earth and go to be in that joyful land where I will reside with You and You will care for my needs. It will be my new "home base."

Until then, help me to fall asleep peacefully tonight so that I can properly care for the body You've given me for now.

I ask these things in Jesus' name. Amen.

THE BALANCE OF SLEEP

A little sleep, a little slumber, a little folding of the
hands to rest, and poverty will come upon you
like a robber, and want like an armed man.
PROVERBS 24:33–34 ESV

God Jehovah, when Jesus was on earth, He walked many places. As a traveling rabbi, He walked and taught His disciples as they went from village to village. This practice brought Him into contact with many people. We know He needed rest for His human body and mind. And there were times when He secluded Himself to find rest and to pray to His Father.

The Proverbs writer informs us through the inspiration of the Holy Spirit that a person can spend too much time resting. And if we do, poverty overtakes us. Where nothing is coming in, the amount going out inevitably decreases.

I want to be like Jesus and know the proper balance of rest and work and leisure. Our enemy, the devil, wants to cloak his suggestions so they seem good, but we know how he works, and we can run to Jesus to help us.

Thank You, Lord, for giving us tools to regulate our internal balance and to help us know when we're sleeping too much.

Amen.

A PETITION FOR HEALTH

Is anyone among you suffering? Let him pray.
Is anyone cheerful? Let him sing praise. Is anyone among
you sick? Let him call for the elders of the church, and
let them pray over him, anointing him with oil in the
name of the Lord. And the prayer of faith will save
the one who is sick, and the Lord will raise him up.
And if he has committed sins, he will be forgiven.
JAMES 5:13–15 ESV

Heavenly Father, sometimes I'm sick in body. It's part of the curse that we just don't feel well now and then. And when times like these come, we don't sleep well. I dread those nights when a tickle in my throat or nausea in my stomach keeps me awake.

Your Word says the prayer of faith will save the sick. I believe the prayer of faith can also help me sleep. This doesn't mean, of course, that every time I'm sick I can escape the consequences of human living. But it does mean that You care about how I feel and how I sleep.

I ask You to help me understand Your Word in a fuller, deeper way so that I can apply it correctly to my life situations. The next time I feel sick in the night, I will pray to You. I might not be healed immediately, but I know that Your presence with me will make a difference to me.

Amen.

SLEEP FOR THE UNCOMFORTABLE

And when they had inflicted many blows upon them,
they threw them into prison, ordering the jailer to
keep them safely. Having received this order, he put
them into the inner prison and fastened their feet in the
stocks. About midnight Paul and Silas were praying
and singing hymns to God, and the prisoners were
listening to them, and suddenly there was a great
earthquake, so that the foundations of the prison
were shaken. And immediately all the doors were
opened, and everyone's bonds were unfastened.
ACTS 16:23–26 ESV

. . . .

Lord Jehovah, sometimes earthquakes happen in the night when Your people praise You!

Paul and Silas turned a night of discomfort into a night of miracles. They were beaten and put into stocks which held them in rigid, painful positions. But they chose to focus on the one who was with them in their discomfort. And that made all the difference.

There will be times in my life when I'm mistreated by others or perhaps in pain, and sleep will be far from me. In those moments, O Lord, help me to choose to praise You for Your presence and grace and strength. In those circumstances, my offering of praise will be the best rest I get.

Please be with me now, Lord, as I close my eyes in sleep. Amen.

WATCHING AND WAITING

*I would have lost heart, unless I had believed that I
would see the goodness of the LORD in the land of the
living. Wait on the LORD; be of good courage, and He
shall strengthen your heart; wait, I say, on the LORD!*
PSALM 27:13–14 NKJV

. . . .

Father in heaven, there have been times when I've had to
sleep in a hospital room. Sometimes it was my own, but
other times, it was the room of a loved one. Watching and
waiting through the night is a difficult thing. No one rests
well, and time drags on and on.

Teach me, Lord, to take life one moment at a time, especially when I'm waiting in a hospital room. Show me how to
have a heart that looks to You instead of my surroundings.
Let me encourage the one with whom I'm waiting and
remember that only You can give me courage.

Lord, work Your grace in my life so that the next time
I must spend a night in the hospital, I'm prepared to look
to You in every wee hour of the morning.

Amen.

WARM SLEEP FOR ALL

" 'The LORD bless you, O home of justice, and mountain of holiness!' And there shall dwell in Judah itself, and in all its cities together, farmers and those going out with flocks. For I have satiated the weary soul, and I have replenished every sorrowful soul." After this I awoke and looked around, and my sleep was sweet to me.
JEREMIAH 31:23–26 NKJV

. . . .

Lord of heaven, when you brought the Hebrews back from their captivity, they slept in sweet peace. They were dwelling in a good land; things were blossoming and industry was vibrant, families were reunited and food was plentiful. Hopeful times make for wonderful sleep.

Sometimes, Lord, we imagine that nothing good will ever come to us, that life is sacrifice and responsibility and routine. And it is. But there are also those parts where You give us warm and fulfilling hours leading to rest that refreshes our souls.

My favorite way to sleep, Lord, is in my familiar bed with good things happening in my family and community, with plenty to eat and good health all around. This doesn't always happen, but I'm asking You to help me praise You for the warm and cozy places in my life. I am blessed.

Amen.

PAIN NO MORE

"And God will wipe away every tear from their eyes; there shall be no more death, nor sorrow, nor crying. There shall be no more pain, for the former things have passed away."

REVELATION 21:4 NKJV

. . . .

Lord Jesus, this verse brings comfort to my heart and mind. One day, there will be no more pain. On this earth, we struggle with disease and disorders, with maladies and conditions. But in heaven, all these things will be gone.

As I head toward my bed this night, I'm happy to think of the eternal world where I will dwell with You and where the sickness and pain of this life will be done.

I pray tonight for those who are experiencing great pain in the night. Be close to them right now, Lord, and bring them comfort and sleep. I pray for persecuted believers in other lands who are unable to sleep tonight because they are in prison or are being tortured. O God, give them grace to endure in Your name.

Tonight, I commit my fellow Christians into Your hands and ask that You would keep us in love and fellowship with You until that great day!

Amen.

WHEN SLEEPLESSNESS COMES

Give not [unnecessary] sleep to your eyes,
nor slumber to your eyelids; deliver yourself,
as a roe or gazelle from the hand of the hunter,
and as a bird from the hand of the fowler.
PROVERBS 6:4–5 AMPC

God in heaven, sometimes I feel I could sleep forever, and other times it seems I will never get to sleep. When I'm not sleepy, it's hard to get the rest my body needs. I know I can come to You with this because You know everything about me. You created me. And when You walked on this earth, You no doubt experienced all the things that I experience in a human body.

Tonight, Lord, I will turn my sleeplessness into fruitfulness by praying for my friends and my family and those whom I know have needs. This is one good outcome of struggling with insomnia. I pray that You would be near to those I've mentioned and that their night would be blessed and restful.

As I finally drift off to sleep for a few hours, I commit the coming day and everything in it to You. You are the God of both day and night.

Amen.

THE UNREST OF CAREGIVING

For God is not unrighteous to forget or overlook your labor and the love which you have shown for His name's sake in ministering to the needs of the saints (His own consecrated people), as you still do. But we do [strongly and earnestly] desire for each of you to show the same diligence and sincerity [all the way through] in realizing and enjoying the full assurance and development of [your] hope until the end.
HEBREWS 6:10–11 AMPC

. . . .

Heavenly Father, because You have cared for me, I will accept my responsibility to care for others. Caregiving requires sacrifice and steadfastness and the ability to see beyond today.

Caregiving is an offering of love to You, the Creator, and to the one who is receiving care. When nothing can be given in return (no money or gifts or even a "thank you"), then it is a true gift of service.

Sleep is fleeting when you're sitting up in the night with another. It's difficult to care for your own needs in that situation. But You give grace, and these times don't last forever. Tonight, as I remember that I may be called upon to render care to someone else, I put that possibility into Your hands and ask You to prepare me for that day.

Amen.

THE ANSWER TO EXHAUSTION

"For I will satisfy the weary soul, and every languishing soul I will replenish."
JEREMIAH 31:25 ESV

. . . .

Jehovah God, I often feel exhausted as I go about my duties and responsibilities. Life is so full, and rest is so fleeting. I'm learning that I need to establish a routine so that the important things in life get done.

The Bible tells us that You will minister to the weary soul. You care about the inward person and outward person. You don't neglect either. When I call on You, You have perfect wisdom and great power. You renew my spirit and let me sleep to renew my body and its processes.

I praise You because You are mighty and good and every kind of rest I need can be found in You. The Bible is filled with examples of those who found their source of continuing strength in You despite overwhelming circumstances—Noah, Abraham, David, John the Baptist, Paul, and more. You were faithful to them in their need, and You will be faithful to me in mine.

I love You, Lord. Amen.

OUR VICTOR OVER DEATH

*God, who saved us and called us to a holy calling,
not because of our works but because of his own
purpose and grace, which he gave us in Christ Jesus
before the ages began, and which now has been
manifested through the appearing of our Savior
Christ Jesus, who abolished death and brought life
and immortality to light through the gospel.*
2 TIMOTHY 1:8–10 ESV

. . . .

Dear Lord, it's difficult to sleep after spending an evening
at the funeral home where a loved one has been laid out
for the final respects of friends and family. Those kinds of
evenings aren't very conducive to the peace and calm we
crave at night-time.

What helps me to keep the proper perspective is to
remember that Jesus has conquered death and it has no
more dominion over us. We may still die an earthly death,
but spiritually, death can never touch us. This truth gives us
comfort as we murmur words of thanks and then go home
to wait for the next day's memorial service.

As my eyes close in sleep tonight, I'm focusing the gaze
of my mind and emotions on You. I'm remembering that
Jesus is the victor over death and the grave.

Amen.

PRAYERS FOR THE FAMILY

*For everything there is a season, and a time for
every matter under heaven. . .a time to laugh.*
ECCLESIASTES 3:1, 4 ESV

A feast is made for laughter.
ECCLESIASTES 10:19 KJV

. . . .

Dear Father God, when my family gets together—my
extended family—we get kind of crazy. We stay up late
and tell funny stories; we raid the refrigerator and play
practical jokes on each other. There is always energy and
life, always something going on, always someone going
somewhere, cooking something, talking with someone,
and on and on.

I'm glad to have these family times. They remind me that
I have roots and that I need to be thankful for the support
of my family. Of course, there are other times when some
of my family members irritate me—please help me in those
moments to draw on Your grace to stay sweet and kind.

When family members show a careless or condescend-
ing attitude toward me, help me not to take it to heart but
to respond as Jesus would.

After these family events, I know a little better how to
pray for my extended family, and I come away reminded
of how very much all of us need Your power in our lives.

Thank You, Lord, for the gift of family. I leave them in
Your hands tonight.

Amen.

AFTER A HARD DAY'S WORK

There is nothing better for a person than that he should eat and drink and find enjoyment in his toil. This also, I saw, is from the hand of God.
ECCLESIASTES 2:24 ESV

. . . .

God of heaven, work is a gift from You. You planned that human beings would have tasks to perform even before there was sin in the world. The first man and woman tended to the perfect garden. And everyone since has had something to do, something to accomplish. We are happiest when we have a purpose.

As I get ready for sleep, I can think back over my day and see how You helped me with my challenges. I give You the praise for helping me find solutions to problems and for giving me the grace to speak kindly to those who were hard to get along with. I praise You for the physical ability to work and for the opportunity to make a living. Help me to be respectful toward my employer, to be amiable with my coworkers, and to be generous with the funds You give me as a result of my job.

The wise writer of Ecclesiastes was inspired to say that finding enjoyment in "toil" is a gift. He was right. And tonight, I praise You for it.

Amen.

WHY WE SLEEP

*Be gracious to me, O LORD, for I am languishing;
heal me, O LORD, for my bones are troubled.*
PSALM 6:2 ESV

....

Heavenly Father, there are days when I feel the words of this psalm. Like David, I languish and my bones feel troubled. After a difficult day of working and serving others or even just taking care of the details of life, my feet hurt and my back aches—even my bones hurt!

It's hard to sleep when you don't feel well, but I need to try. Nothing can restore the body like a good night of rest. You made sleep to be rejuvenating and refreshing. Forgive me for the times when I've abused my body by giving it little sleep and then expecting it to perform without fail for me. I know that someday this carelessness will catch up with me; I want to begin to be a good steward now.

Thank You, Father, for loving me when I feel good and when I don't. Thank You for being the source of my abiding peace. Even when my body is weary, my soul is at rest.

Amen.

BAD DAYS REDEEMED

The LORD will fulfill his purpose for me;
your steadfast love, O LORD, endures forever.
Do not forsake the work of your hands.
PSALM 138:8 ESV

O Lord, when I have difficulty on the job, it carries over into the other aspects of my life. I feel like a failure, insignificant, unworthy, and depressed. I like to succeed at what I do, and I like to feel organized and settled in my assignments.

The worst kind of day is when I'm reprimanded by my supervisor or even fired. The humiliation is bad enough, but the deep feeling of inadequacy haunts me for a long time. I think it's hard on all of us to face our inabilities and inferiorities. The only way to deal with them properly is to know the truth about who we are in Christ and to realize that correcting our errors and moving ahead in His direction is what will put us back on track.

Tonight, I'm asking You to be my help as I deal with the aftermath of work today. Help me to remember, in my review, that You can redeem anything I bring to You and that You will continue to mature me in grace.

In Jesus' name, amen.

PRAYING AND TURNING
THE OTHER CHEEK

But I say to you, Do not resist the evil man [who
injures you]; but if anyone strikes you on the right
jaw or cheek, turn to him the other one too.
MATTHEW 5:39 AMPC

. . . .

Lord Jesus, many things in this life are unpleasant and painful. Animosity from others is one of those things. I don't
think I've ever been slapped by someone who was angry
with me, but there have been times when words have felt
like a slap in the face.

Some people have the ability to use their words like
weapons, cutting down whoever is in their way. When
that happens, I have a choice about what to do next. I can
obey the voice of the Holy Spirit, or I can choose to obey
the voice of self.

The voice of self screams at me to get even, to slap the
person back, to throw stinging words back at them, to find
a way to make them pay.

But Jesus says, "Love your enemies." And He tells us
to return good when someone does evil to us. It's counter-
intuitive, but it's the principle of the heavenly kingdom.

As I get ready for bed tonight, I bring to You my hurtful moments and ask for grace to process them correctly.
Thank You that I can be victorious through Christ.

Amen.

WHEN I AM PERSECUTED

"Blessed are you when others revile you and persecute you and utter all kinds of evil against you falsely on my account. Rejoice and be glad, for your reward is great in heaven, for so they persecuted the prophets who were before you."
MATTHEW 5:11–12 ESV

Dear Father God, when I've read these verses before, I haven't thought about the fact that persecution can be many things. I've imagined it as referring to Christian martyrs and those imprisoned for Christ in other countries. And it definitely does include those situations.

But I think it might also refer to circumstances where a Christ-follower is being mistreated because of the stand that that person takes on a moral or ethical issue. And that reminds me that I am a true citizen not of this world, but rather of the one to come.

As I look ahead to tomorrow, I shouldn't be surprised when my biblically based views on current events or my manner of living is thought peculiar by others. I should expect that. And it should, conversely, make me happy to realize that, by Your grace, I know Your ways. Help me never to become cynical toward sinners but to do my best to share the light I have found with them as You give me opportunity and wisdom.

In Jesus' name, amen.

A RESPONSE TO SLANDER

*But in your hearts honor Christ the Lord as holy, always
being prepared to make a defense to anyone who asks
you for a reason for the hope that is in you; yet do it
with gentleness and respect, having a good conscience,
so that, when you are slandered, those who revile
your good behavior in Christ may be put to shame.*
1 PETER 3:15–16 ESV

. . . .

Lord God, it's painful to discover that someone has spread false stories about me or said things about me that have injured my reputation. When this happens, the natural human response is to get even by doing the same to the perpetrator.

But Your Word instructs me not to behave as the unregenerate do. And You have promised to give me the grace to follow through!

The Christian response is to make sure I have answers when others ask me questions and to go about my daily life in a godly manner so that when someone slanders me, the track record of my life puts them to shame. In that case, all who know me would tend to doubt the truth of the slanderer's tales. A lifetime of upright living can cancel out the lies.

As I think about tomorrow and what it may bring, I have confidence that following Your Word will always point my life along the right path.

Thank You, Lord. Amen.

UNINTERRUPTED SLEEP

*It is in vain that you rise up early and go
late to rest, eating the bread of anxious
toil; for he gives to his beloved sleep.*
PSALM 127:2 ESV

. . . .

Dear Heavenly Father, there are times in my life when sleep is difficult. Sickness or tragedy or anxiety causes me to be wakeful, to toss and turn, and to feel very unrested the next morning.

I know that You are the giver of all good things, and sleep is one of those gifts. Tonight, I pray that You would grant me a good night of rest. Help the pathways of my mind not to be frantic but to be brimming with the promises of Your Word that I have stored in my heart. Give my mind and body rest, dim the distractions, and lull me to deep sleep so that I can be ready for my day tomorrow.

When I have difficult nights of unrest, I'm reminded to have compassion for those who suffer from debilitating diseases and disorders or who have horrific home conditions or who have been through great loss—all of these circumstances can interrupt the natural and needed cycles of sleep. Help me never to become callous to human extremity.

Thank You, God, that You care about everything in my life, even sleep. I commit this night to You.

Amen.

SLEEPING WITH THE LIGHT ON

For thou art my lamp, O LORD: and the
LORD will lighten my darkness.
2 SAMUEL 22:29 KJV

. . . .

Lord Jehovah, when I was a little girl, I liked to have a light on in my room. I was worried about all the sounds I heard in the house and about all the things my imagination could create. Keeping a light on seemed to keep the monsters at bay.

Now that I'm grown, I know that the night doesn't automatically create scary things, but I still find that the darkness makes my fears worse. A night-light won't take them away, but I know You can help me deal with them.

You are the lamp that shines in my night-time. And You are the one who lightens the midnight of my anxieties. I turn to You as I get into my bed tonight. I bring to You all the shadowy unknowns and ask You to calm me with Your light of truth and hope and faithfulness.

I ask these things in Jesus' name, believing that You will do it.

Amen.

SLEEPING IN
CROWDED CONDITIONS

I will give great praise and thanks to the Lord with my mouth; yes, and I will praise Him among the multitude.
PSALM 109:30 AMPC

. . . .

Lord, sometimes I feel like I'm trying to sleep amid a multitude!

When I have company at my home and the hallways and bathrooms and kitchen are crowded, it feels like we live in a space without walls. We do things not as individuals, but as a unit. We must work around one another. We must think about the other. We must bear with one another.

It isn't easy to rest in these conditions, but it's a reminder to all of us that we live not for our own gratification, but for Yours. Sometimes You call us to sacrifice our comfort for others.

I can praise You in the midst of the people around me by the way I graciously bear with them when they get in my way. You have given the gift of family to me, and I'm glad they feel welcome in my home. Let me be a considerate hostess who puts others' needs before my own.

When my company has gone home, You will give me rest. And the memories will last a lifetime.

In Jesus' name, amen.

THE NIGHT WORLD

And God made the two great lights—the greater light
(the sun) to rule the day and the lesser light (the
moon) to rule the night. He also made the stars.
GENESIS 1:16 AMPC

. . . .

Creator God, thank You for making the night world.

When I have an opportunity to be still and watch the things that happen at night, I'm awed by Your handiwork. You are the master designer of all the beauty and splendor of the night sky. The sun retires to his other hemisphere and the moon emerges from her dressing room to illuminate the landscape. The stars gradually appear to my eyes, although I know they are there all the time, glowing in the heavens that You continually behold.

When human beings take the opportunity to sleep outside, whether camping or in a backyard hammock, we're reminded again of the wonder of the world You brought into being. Help me always to remember that the theory of evolution denies the power of a Creator, that it puts the genius of the created world up to chance. Something in my very nature knows, deep down, that such an occurrence is impossible. Those lights in the heavens could never create themselves.

As I bring my day to a close, I know that nothing in my life is too difficult for You, the one who crafted the moon and spun the stars.

I love You, Lord. Amen.

LOOKING AHEAD TO
A DAY OF REST

*And on the seventh day God ended His work
which He had done; and He rested on the seventh
day from all His work which He had done.*
GENESIS 2:2 AMPC

So the people rested on the seventh day.
EXODUS 16:30 AMPC

. . . .

Dear Father God, thank You for creating a day of rest in the week. From the beginning, You established the pattern of one day of rest in seven. In the Old Testament, You hallowed the seventh day; seven is the number of perfection. And while You were not tired, You ceased from work to show us the importance of rest. In the New Testament, after the resurrection of Jesus on the first day of the week, Christians began to meet for worship; it was the sanctified and set-apart day.

I'm glad to have a day when I'm commanded to rest. It's easy to let other activities and demands spill over into times usually reserved for downtime, but knowing that observing a day of rest is one of the Ten Commandments helps me to be intentional about it. I make a commitment to honor You by resting on Your day.

As I think about the week ahead of me, I know the day of rest will be welcome. And I will honor You with it.

Amen.

FALLING ASLEEP
WHEN I'M TIRED

Behold, He who keeps Israel will
neither slumber nor sleep.
PSALM 121:4 AMPC

. . . .

Dear Father, sometimes I fall asleep in the car. Not while I'm driving, but when I'm traveling with others. The hum of the motor and the forward motion of the vehicle, together with the tiredness I'm feeling from my day-to-day life, lull me into napping. I'm subject to my human fatigue; the response of sleep is one my body is quick to take when it's tired.

But You are not like me. You never get tired or need to sleep. There is never a moment when You doze off because You've had a lot going on. You never feel like taking a nap or resting Your eyes. You are constantly aware of the details of my life, and You never grow weary, whether day or night.

As I think about Your greatness, I'm comforted tonight while I get ready to enter the world of sleep that You created for me. I'm glad that You are God and Father and the sustainer of all. I'm Your creation, and I rest in Your authority and sovereignty tonight.

Thank You, Lord. Amen.

SLEEPING AND WAKING

I lay down and slept; I woke again,
for the LORD sustained me.
PSALM 3:5 ESV

. . . .

Lord God, I've heard of people who can awaken at any time without an alarm. I don't think I'm one of those people, but I admire that ability. I have even slept through my alarms, so I definitely need help getting up at a certain time.

Waking up from sleep is a process all in itself. I don't know all the scientific explanations for what takes place, but I do know that You are the one who allows my eyes to open and my brain to register the fact that another day has begun. You give me the self-awareness of where I am and what is happening in the day ahead. As I grow older, I may have more difficulty remembering some of those things, but the fact that I can know them at all is a testament to Your creative work.

In the morning, I'll thank You for causing me to awaken and for keeping my heart beating and my lungs breathing and my blood circulating while I slept. Right now, I thank You for the memories of yesterday and the promise of tomorrow. As I go to sleep tonight, I can anticipate the moment when I awaken in the morning, knowing You will give me strength for all that takes place.

I praise You, Lord! Amen.

The Serenity of Sleep

SLEEP IN DELIGHT

But his delight is in the law of the LORD,
and on his law he meditates day and night.
PSALM 1:2 ESV

• •

Heavenly Father, Your Word tells me that I can find delight in meditating on Your truth.

As I go to sleep tonight, I know that I can experience delight and rest by remembering Your Word as my mind shuts down for the night. And I can have the promise of delight for tomorrow if I take time to look into Your law in the morning.

Nothing is more important than knowing what is true and what I need to do to please You. I ask You, Lord, to guide me as I study Your Word tomorrow, to give me eyes to discern and a heart that accepts what I learn. Let the Holy Spirit illuminate for me the deep things of Your Word.

Lord, many sleeping pills and potions are on the market, but the best sleep aid is found in the Word You have preserved down through the generations. Thank You that I have a copy in my home.

Now, Lord, I will take a minute to remember a specific promise and to breathe a prayer for tomorrow. Then I can sleep in delight.

Amen.

BEAUTY SLEEP

*And let the beauty of the L*ORD *our God be upon*
us, and establish the work of our hands for
us; yes, establish the work of our hands.
PSALM 90:17 NKJV

. . . .

O Lord, we speak about getting our "beauty sleep." And it's true that adequate rest is needed for the body to look its best and perform in optimum ways. A lack of sleep will affect the brightness of the eyes, the luster of the skin, and other aspects of appearance. You made us to need rest to rejuvenate our bodies; and since sin entered the world, the negative effects of gravity and aging create even more of a struggle for us!

But I've found that the best kind of beauty sleep comes from aligning my will with Yours and committing myself to You for a night of rest. You keep me from having the struggles of a guilty conscience or an obsession with the problems of tomorrow. You give me the rest I need when I bring my night, as well as my day, to You.

Now, as I pull up my quilt, I'm confident in the knowledge that You do all things well and that You will beautify my soul as it rests in You.

Amen.

LOOKING AHEAD TO TOMORROW

Do not boast of [yourself and] tomorrow,
for you know not what a day may bring forth.
PROVERBS 27:1 AMPC

. . . .

Father, when I go to sleep, I like to think ahead to tomorrow and try to plan what I need to do. I know it's good to be purposeful about my living. But at the same time, You don't want me to be presumptive about my earthly life. I can't assume that I know how everything should go or what will happen in Your will. Only You know how You have determined to accomplish Your plans and glorify Your name.

Lord, I do look forward to the good things of my life. I know that a new day will bring Your faithfulness and care, the love of my family, and the simple pleasures of food and color and music and friends. But I don't want to focus on the emergencies that might come or the challenges I will face.

Lord, I'm assured that whatever tomorrow brings, Your grace will enable me to overcome. And so I anticipate the new day, not boasting in my control of it but resting in Your design of it.

In Jesus' name, amen.

BLESSED WITH BLISS

*The Lord lives! Blessed be my Rock;
and let the God of my salvation be exalted.*
PSALM 18:46 AMPC

. . . .

Dear Father God, I'm discovering that when I trust in You, every night can be a spa for the soul. Every stretch of sleep can be bliss, a blessed few hours.

Day spas are very popular with my friends. There are conversations about getting therapeutic massages or being pampered with beauty treatments and similar means of relaxation and body care. Women, who work hard in their homes and for their families and often hold an outside job as well, respond with sighs of bliss to these kinds of pleasures. And nothing is wrong with caring for the body, soothing the stress of daily life, and even beautifying ourselves within the boundaries of Your principles in scripture.

But the best day spa of all is a focus on and a commitment to You. As I grasp hold of this truth, even at night, my tomorrows become better and better.

You are alive! You are my rock! You are the God of my salvation!

This is true, life-changing bliss.

Amen.

FILTERING IDEAS BEFORE I SLEEP

*Then I saw that there is more gain in wisdom
than in folly, as there is more gain in light than
in darkness. The wise person has his eyes in
his head, but the fool walks in darkness.*
ECCLESIASTES 2:13–14 ESV

. . . .

Holy Lord, tonight as I drift off to sleep, I'm thinking of new ideas for tomorrow. My head is filled with thoughts of things I can do and things I need to do. I'm also pondering ideas that have come to me through reading news articles and books this past week; some of them align with Your Word, and some of them are the opposite of who You are and how You work.

These verses from the divinely inspired pen of the wisdom writer remind me that a discerning woman has spiritual eyes that really "see" what is true in all the ideas she hears. I want to be that kind of woman. I don't want to be a foolish woman who walks in darkness.

Father, You are the one from whom all good and true ideas flow. Help me to hear the voice of Your Holy Spirit as I think about what I've read and what I need to apply to my tomorrow.

In Jesus' name, amen.

PLANNING AND SAVING

Go to the ant, O sluggard; consider her ways, and be wise. Without having any chief, officer, or ruler, she prepares her bread in summer and gathers her food in harvest.
PROVERBS 6:6–8 ESV

. . . .

Holy Father, Your Word teaches the principle of preparing for the future. While You don't want us to worry about our food or clothing or obsess about our to-do list for tomorrow, You do teach us that those who are wise practice the disciplines of saving and storing. We are not to be careless people, using up our provisions today and not even thinking about the days to come.

You inspired the writer of Proverbs to remind us of the little ant and the way she busies herself with her home preparations. There is a principle here that all of us can understand. We are not to be wasteful or slothful. We are not to be focused solely on the pleasure of today.

Help me, Lord, to think about tomorrow with wisdom. Show me ways that I can put back money for my later years. Help me to identify ways I can be a better steward of the funds You give me. Guide me as I think about what to keep in storage and what to give away.

I trust You to guide all my planning, Lord. Amen.

PROMISES TO SLEEP ON

In hope of eternal life, which God, who never lies,
promised before the ages began.
TITUS 1:2 ESV

. . . .

Lord Jesus, thank You that I can look ahead to tomorrow with hope because of Your promises. There is nothing I will face this week that You cannot meet with Your strength and power. And the most important promise of all is the promise that those who have trusted in You for salvation have the hope of eternal life.

All the daily struggles I face look less traumatic when I remember that I am made for eternity, and the things that really matter are loving You and loving others. The problems I'm facing in my job and the little irritations in my daily routine are not things I should fret over as I go to sleep. I need to see them through the lens of eternal value, and then they will shrink and take their proper perspective.

Father, tomorrow is a fresh day, not yet given to me but for which I should prepare if You ordain it. Overarching everything is the certainty of eternal life in Your heaven.

Thank You, Lord. Amen.

THE COUNSEL OF DREAMS

For when dreams increase and words grow many,
there is vanity; but God is the one you must fear.
ECCLESIASTES 5:7 ESV

. . . .

Dear Lord, sometimes I have dreams that scare me. In the night, they seem so real. The images they bring before my mind are disturbing, sometimes tragic and heartbreaking. I awaken with a start, thankful, as awareness sets in, that it was all a story that my mind made up.

The wisdom writer was divinely inspired to warn us against putting stock in dreams and visions. There are those today who would say that every dream means something, but of course we know that Your Word trumps anything a person may dream. And Your Holy Spirit only speaks counsel to us that agrees with the words in scripture. This helps me safeguard my soul against error.

Father, You don't want us to be dependent on dreams as we make decisions about the future. You want us to take counsel from the Bible and time spent with You. If we fear You with a holy reverence, You will show us the next step today. Sometimes you work through impressions and even through dreams, but I must be careful to check those messages against the words You have spoken. Please give me wisdom in my decision-making, Lord.

In Jesus' name, amen.

SENSITIVITY IN MY DEALINGS TOMORROW

Only, may the LORD grant you discretion and understanding, that when he gives you charge over Israel you may keep the law of the LORD your God. Then you will prosper if you are careful to observe the statutes and the rules that the LORD commanded Moses for Israel.

1 CHRONICLES 22:12–13 ESV

. . . .

Father in heaven, one of the gifts You will give me for tomorrow is a heart that is sensitive and discerning. King David uttered these words to his son Solomon as he prepared him for the work he would do in his lifetime. But they also apply to me through the principle on which they are built. If I'm careful to observe the statutes in Your Word and follow You in obedience, I will be blessed with the discernment I need in my daily life.

Tomorrow, I will face situations in which I need wisdom higher than my own. I ask You right now, tonight, to guide my thoughts and my words. Help me to be sensitive to the feelings of others as I speak. Show me how to use truth well—not as a bludgeon, but as a light. Check my spirit when I start to say something that would bring reproach on You. Enlighten my understanding by Your Holy Spirit so that I may glorify You.

I ask these things in Jesus' name. Amen.

LIGHT IN MY SOUL

But if we walk in the light, as he is in the light,
we have fellowship one with another, and the blood
of Jesus Christ his Son cleanseth us from all sin.
1 John 1:7 kjv

. . . .

Lord Jesus, I sleep best when it's dark outside. I know there are some places on earth where it stays light a long time during certain seasons, and I'm sure I would learn to sleep in that setting, but it's much easier for me to fall asleep when it's dark.

Yet, in my soul, I always want to be flooded with light. I never want the darkness of sin and deception to dominate my inmost being. Even while I'm sleeping, I want the inside of me to be blazing with light.

The way to achieve this ongoing soul light is to walk in obedience to You, knowing that the blood of Jesus keeps me clean. And then I don't have to fear if something should happen to me in the middle of the night—if tragedy should strike or death should come. I'm always ready when Your light rules in my soul.

If there is any way in which I'm not following You in obedience, Lord, please show me so that I can confess and forsake it. Your light means more to me than anything.

In Jesus' name, amen.

THE AROMA OF CHRIST IN ME

*For we are a fragrance of Christ to God among those who
are being saved and among those who are perishing.*
2 CORINTHIANS 2:15 NASB

. . . .

Dear Father God, tonight I'm thinking about fragrances and the way they affect me. Certain aromas and flavors are supposed to promote sleep. Chamomile tea is touted for its drowsiness-inducing effect. Lavender oil is said to have a calming effect. These and other fragrances are things we can try to help us drop off into a restful sleep.

But the best fragrance of all is the aroma of Christ in me as I follow You. Then, whether I'm awake or asleep, You are glorified in my being and others can see the work You have done for me.

I ask You, Lord, to guide me tomorrow in what I say and do so that Your fragrance might be dispensed through me in whatever setting I enter. Let me respond to others with restraint and kindness. Let me be diligent in my work and edifying in my relationships. I thank You for all that You're teaching me about wholeheartedly following You.

In Jesus' name, amen.

AN OPEN HEART

"I delight to do Your will, my God;
Your Law is within my heart."
PSALM 40:8 NASB

. . . .

Dear Father God, as I think about my week and what I need to do when I wake up, I ask that You would increase the openness of my heart as I determine to follow You. I want to be like the psalmist who delighted in following You. Let that be the cry of my heart as well.

There are things about Your will for my week that I don't know yet; but when I discover them, I want my first response to be surrender and acceptance and even an embrace of what You have ordained.

I bring to You, Lord, my to-do list and my relationships and my possessions. In all of these things, I want to be open to Your leading. It's hard for me to take my hands off, but I open them before You and ask You to show me what to do. And I know that tomorrow will be better because of it.

I love You, Lord. Amen.

THE BLESSING OF FAITH

*So then those who are of faith are
blessed with believing Abraham.*
GALATIANS 3:9 NKJV

. . . .

Lord Almighty, one of the gifts of serenity is a faith that holds on and won't let go. Please keep developing this kind of faith in me. I want my faith to be like that of Abraham. I want to be unwavering in my belief that You will come through, that You have a purpose that is higher than I can see, that You are in control of all things that concern me.

Abraham left his home to move to an unknown destination. He trusted You for descendants when he was old and his wife was barren. He refused to give up on the promises he heard from You.

Tomorrow and for the rest of my life, Lord, there will be moments and situations in which I can't see You working. But please give me the faith to believe that You are—faithfully, steadily, wonderfully.

To have this kind of faith is not only a goal but a gift. To live with faith in God is a blessing, and I'm thankful for it tonight as I lie down to sleep.

Amen.

GOOD WORDS

A word fitly spoken and in due season is
like apples of gold in settings of silver.
PROVERBS 25:11 AMPC

. . . .

Dear Lord, words, once spoken, don't go away. They remain in the memory of the hearer and are noted by You in Your record books. Jesus said that we will give an accounting for every idle word we speak (Matthew 12:36). That warning motivates me to be careful in my speech. I don't want to dishonor You here, and I don't want the record books to reveal sinful words when I'm there.

Yet, Proverbs tells me that I can speak good words, and they will be one of the blessings of a serene life. I want my mouth to be accustomed to edifying, truthful, and beautiful speech. I want my native language to be Yours—the truth of heaven.

Thank You for promising to help us when we put ourselves in Your hands. Tonight, as I think about tomorrow, I ask You to be with me and let my conversations be filled with the best words, like golden apples framed in silver settings—rich, lovely, and always appropriate.

Thank You, Jesus. Amen.

FULL ASSURANCE

Let us all come forward and draw near with true (honest and sincere) hearts in unqualified assurance and absolute conviction engendered by faith (by that leaning of the entire human personality on God in absolute trust and confidence in His power, wisdom, and goodness), having our hearts sprinkled and purified from a guilty (evil) conscience and our bodies cleansed with pure water.
HEBREWS 10:22 AMP

. . . .

O Lord, the world around me is looking for assurance. All around me people are scurrying about, collecting material possessions, grappling for high-paying jobs, boasting of their children's accomplishments, envying their friends, and generally not enjoying a life of meaning. They don't have the assurance that their lives matter. They feel guilt for their sins, whether they really know it or not. That is what causes the unrest and lack of peace.

I know I can face tomorrow with the assurance that I'm Your child because I have opened my heart to Your redemptive power and confessed that I fully trust in You. You can redeem my past and transform my tomorrow. As I prepare for sleep, I draw near to You in full assurance of faith because my heart is cleansed, my conscience is purified, and my future is settled.

Thank You, Lord Jesus. Amen.

EXPECTING GOOD
THINGS AHEAD

*So shall you know skillful and godly Wisdom
to be thus to your life; if you find it, then shall
there be a future and a reward, and your hope
and expectation shall not be cut off.*
PROVERBS 24:14 AMPC

. . . .

Heavenly Father, the joy of expectation is one of the delights of looking ahead. I like to have things to anticipate—the holidays with all their beauty and family togetherness, vacations filled with travel and new experiences and a change of pace, days spent in the quiet of my home with a quilt and a good book, and so much more. The greatest expectation of all is the reality of heaven when I die. That expectation keeps all the others in proper perspective. And keeping the hope of heaven in mind adds wisdom to my life.

Tonight, I'm thinking of the expectations I have for this coming week, and I want to make sure that You are honored in all my plans. Looking forward to things without You negates my very reason for existing. Thank You that You have promised never to leave me or forsake me. If I will honor You, You will bless what I do for eternal good.

Amen.

CHRIST MY FOUNDATION

Thou wilt keep him in perfect peace, whose mind is stayed on thee: because he trusteth in thee. Trust ye in the LORD for ever: for in the LORD JEHOVAH is everlasting strength.
ISAIAH 26:3–4 KJV

. . . .

O Lord, when I've tried in the past to focus my life on anything but You, I've only been frustrated and made a mess of things. Like the parable that Jesus told about the wise man building on a rock, I want the temple of my life to be established squarely on the foundation I have in You. Making anything else supreme is idolatry.

I ask that You would show me how to build my life on You in practical ways. As I go through my day tomorrow, point out to me the ways in which I can honor You and put You first. May a longing to build on Your foundation be the central motive in my decisions and words and actions

I will go to sleep tonight resting in the fact that You are my everlasting strength.

Amen.

A RIGHT CONFIDENCE

*For the Lord shall be your confidence, firm and
strong, and shall keep your foot from being
caught [in a trap or some hidden danger].*
PROVERBS 3:26 AMPC

. . . .

O God my Father, confidence is one of the traits that is
difficult for me. I naturally doubt myself. I question my
abilities. I'm fearful about saying that I know something
for sure and tend to distrust my own judgment.

But I do trust Your judgment. I know that You are the
author, indeed the essence, of all truth and that Your ways
of working are perfect. And so I come to You tonight before
I sleep, claiming the promise of this verse that You will
be my confidence, the very embodiment of confidence
in my life.

Lord, I don't want the earthly kind of confidence,
which really seems to be arrogance—confidence that
only looks out for itself, making sure self always looks
good and is never overlooked. No. Instead, I want *Your*
confidence—which always keeps self and others and You
in proper balance.

Thank You for being my confidence, Lord. In Jesus'
name, amen.

BLAMELESSNESS

And may the God of peace Himself sanctify you
through and through [separate you from profane
things, make you pure and wholly consecrated to
God]; and may your spirit and soul and body be
preserved sound and complete [and found] blameless
at the coming of our Lord Jesus Christ (the Messiah).
1 THESSALONIANS 5:23 AMPC

. . . .

Holy Lord, You have said that I should be holy before You.
You don't ask me to be infallible in my judgment or without human error in everything. But You do call me to be
blameless in motive before You, so that my heart is totally
devoted to doing what pleases You and not me. The apostle Paul was divinely inspired to write that You can sanctify
me and set me apart to have this kind of blameless heart.

Lord, so many people go to sleep with the knowledge
that they are not blameless. They are fearful that others
will discover how they have secretly sinned against them,
broken their covenantal relationships, betrayed their
trust, defrauded them, or committed some other willful
transgression.

But in You, I can be blameless in my soul of all evil
intentions. And I'm so glad I can go to sleep tonight with
that knowledge.

Amen.

THE CALM IN THE STORM

He hushes the storm to a calm and to a gentle
whisper, so that the waves of the sea are still.
PSALM 107:29 AMPC

. . . .

Lord of the storms, when You walked on this earth, you encountered the meteorological kind of storms—and You calmed them with Your voice. Today, You still have the power to calm not only the physical storms but also the emotional and spiritual and mental storms that arise on my horizon.

One of the ways that divine serenity works its blessings in my life is that I can turn to You in my storms and hear Your authoritative voice that brings the wind and waves to a calm. When I'm tossed about by blasts that I didn't even see coming, I need not fear that they are more than You can handle.

Thank You, Lord Jesus, that when You are in the boat, the storms must bow and obey. I know that sometimes You take me through storms instead of taking them away; but in those times, Your presence in the vessel of my life keeps me steady and brings me to the other side.

Thank You for being the God of every storm I face. Amen.

A SENSE OF AWE

"He is your praise. He is your God, who
has done for you these great and terrifying
things that your eyes have seen."
DEUTERONOMY 10:21 ESV

....

Mighty God, You are the God of wonders. The God of miracles. The God who evokes awe in me.

I think of the Old and New Testaments and the wonders You performed in Egypt, at the Red Sea, for David, in the fiery furnace, at the Jordan, at the tomb of Lazarus, and so much more. There is nothing You cannot do. And sometimes You allow us to observe Your might.

One of the blessings of knowing You is living with a sense of awe, this wondrous awareness that I'm a witness to Your great power over and over again. Those who don't know You have only the company of their own logic and the assertions of earthly science. They deny the possibility and reality of Your sovereign being, the truth of Your creative and preservative work in our earth.

Thank You for the privilege of being part of Your family through my faith in Christ. Thank You for showing me in so many ways that You love me. Thank You for the gift of awe.

In Jesus' name, amen.

GOODWILL TOWARD OTHERS TOMORROW

*And above all these [put on] love and enfold
yourselves with the bond of perfectness [which binds
everything together completely in ideal harmony].*
COLOSSIANS 3:14 AMPC

. . . .

O Father, I praise You tonight as I center my thoughts on You before I sleep.

Thank You for the goodwill You put in my heart for others. While some are closer friends to me than others, I know Your Word says I must not harbor resentment or hatred toward anyone. Instead, I leave vengeance with You and walk forward wishing good to all who come across my path. Because I have been given mercy and goodwill, despite my transgressions against You, You call me to reflect You in offering the same to others.

When I arise in the morning and go to my daily tasks, whether working around the house or serving others in ministry or using my body and mind to earn a living on the job, I want to have Your spirit of goodwill permeate my being and guide my words and actions.

When Jesus was on earth, He gave us the example of how to interact with everyone, those who like us and those who don't. Thank You that Your grace enables me to follow His example.

Amen.

A CLEAR CONSCIENCE
AT BEDTIME

I have hope in God, which they themselves also accept,
that there will be a resurrection of the dead, both of the
just and the unjust. This being so, I myself always strive to
have a conscience without offense toward God and men.
ACTS 24:15–16 NKJV

Dear Lord, one of the best aids to a good night's rest is a conscience that doesn't prick me with the memory of hurtful things I've said and done. Thank You that because of Jesus' work in my heart and power in my life, I can keep short accounts in my life. If I offend someone, by Your grace I can make it right immediately and not carry it with me into the evening and night. Thank You for helping me choose not to give in to temptation and forgiving me and empowering me when I realize I've wronged someone and need to apologize.

Lord, the best way for me to keep my conscience clear toward You is to spend time with You daily, learning more about You and Your will and commands. Then my relationship with You and my desire to please You are strengthened.

As I drift off to sleep tonight, I'm grateful for what You've done in my life, and I ask that You would help me glorify You tomorrow.

In Jesus' name, amen.

IN ADORATION OF YOU

How great are His signs, and how mighty His wonders!
His kingdom is an everlasting kingdom, and His
dominion is from generation to generation.
DANIEL 4:3 NKJV

. . . .

Mighty Father, I'm thinking tonight about the wonderful works You have accomplished in my life. And I also remember the incredible wonders You have performed all through human history. The Bible records account after account of the ways You astounded mankind to accomplish Your divine and eternal purpose. You specialize in performing what seems impossible in our eyes. You don't operate in human possibility. You delight in bringing to pass whatever You desire to glorify Your name.

Some in our world go to sleep at night after watching great feats performed by others in sports or science or after reading news accounts of the accomplishments of man in one area or another. But help me to remember Your great deeds, which will endure forever.

Tonight, I lift up my adoration to You, telling You of my love for You and my commitment to serve You all my days. When I awaken in the morning, bring to my mind all the ways my life can be an offering of praise and gratitude back to You.

Amen.

CALLED TO DECLARE

*But it is good for me to draw near to God; I have put my
trust in the Lord GOD, that I may declare all Your works.*
PSALM 73:28 NKJV

. . . .

O God, one of the ways I can glorify You is by giving
testimony to the way You're working in my life. Because
I've put my trust in You and seen You work, I can give a
firsthand account of the love and power to be found in
belonging to You.

You have called me to be Your ambassador, letting
others see what You can do in a life. And this is not to draw
glory to me but rather to You, so that they too can find
fulfillment in being Your child. That's why You want others
to see Your majesty and love. You love the world so much
that You do everything You can in keeping with Your will
and Word to open the eyes of mankind to Your goodness.

Lord, tomorrow, may I think of ways in which I can
declare all Your works. Bring to my mind the ideas and then
provide opportunities for me to follow through.

I trust You, Lord, to guide me in all things.

Amen.

A PRAYER FOR PRUDENCE

*The wise in heart are called prudent, understanding,
and knowing, and winsome speech increases
learning [in both speaker and listener].*
PROVERBS 16:21 AMPC

. . . .

Dear Lord, I'm glad You're teaching me how to live. As I read Your Word and grow in understanding, I see how very much I still need to learn!

I want to be called "wise in heart." I know that those who are foolish resist instruction and scorn restraint. I don't want to fall into those traps. Please keep the eyes of my heart open to truth so I don't become blinded by the world's wisdom.

As I think about all that's in store tomorrow, I know the only way I can live a truly prudent life is to acknowledge You as Lord over every area of my life and commit to following You in all things. Whatever Your Holy Spirit shows me to do, I will obey. Give me a mind that runs quickly to the biblical principle in every situation. And when I come to the end of my day tomorrow, let me commit to following You even more closely the next day.

In Jesus' name, amen.

FOREORDAINED FOR GOOD WORKS

For we are his workmanship, created in Christ
Jesus for good works, which God prepared
beforehand, that we should walk in them.
EPHESIANS 2:10 ESV

. . . .

Dear Heavenly Father, I can trust in You tonight because You know ahead of time what You have planned for me.

Your will is revealed to me day by day, but You already see the end, the finished product, the final result. That idea can be a little scary. You also see if I will turn my back on You, and that thought really makes me nervous! But the fact is that You don't choose for me; You simply know what I will choose. If You didn't, You wouldn't be God. You would be limited like me.

Lord, You have prepared good works for me to do. You have planned for me to glorify You in righteousness. You have planned for me to succeed and not fail. You have planned for me to be a trophy of grace.

No trick of Satan and no action of anyone on earth can thwart what You have ordained if I cooperate with Your grace. You will bring it to pass in my life if I surrender to You.

Tonight, I lay my life before You again and ask You to complete the work that You have begun in and through me.

In Jesus' name, amen.

A SPIRIT OF THANKFULNESS

And let the peace of Christ rule in your hearts, to which indeed you were called in one body. And be thankful.
COLOSSIANS 3:15 ESV

Dear Lord, one important trait for me to develop continually is thankfulness. When I'm thankful for what You've given me, I have a proper perspective of my place in Your kingdom and a humble, usable spirit.

Being humble is the key to knowing You in a personal relationship. I can't come to You if I think I don't need anything from You. And if I don't acknowledge that You have already done so much for me, then I'm not a candidate for Your work in my future.

Thank You, Lord, for calling me from my sin.

Thank You, Lord, for extending mercy to me.

Thank You, Lord, for giving me an inheritance in heaven.

Thank You, Lord, for making a place for me in Your family.

Thank You, Lord, for establishing my feet in Your will.

Thank You, Lord, for setting my eyes on eternity.

Thank You, Lord, that You have all the power I need to live a victorious life until You take me to heaven or return in the clouds.

I praise You!

Amen.

A GOD OF JUSTICE

Thus says the LORD: "Keep justice, and do righteousness, for soon my salvation will come, and my righteousness be revealed. Blessed is the man who does this, and the son of man who holds it fast."
ISAIAH 56:1–2 ESV

. . . .

Father in heaven, You are a God of justice. You hate falsity and deception. You are absolute truth. You don't show partiality.

The first lie of the enemy was to hint that You were unfair, unjust, in restricting Adam and Eve from the tree in the center of the garden. He knew that the seed he planted would take root in the human mind and cause suspicion against the loving Creator.

Today, Satan still works in this way. He likes to insult Your holy name by insinuating that You are unjust, withholding from us the things that would make us happy. He plays with our minds, tempting us to doubt You and offering the empty baubles of self-fulfillment in sinful ways.

But I'm glad You help us discern the lies and maintain our trust in You. Once we've determined to stay committed to You, nothing in heaven or on earth can change that resolve. And we can know for certain that You will do justly. You always have. You always will.

Amen.

A BETTER PURPOSE FOR ME

For the Lord of hosts has purposed, and who will annul it? His hand is stretched out, and who will turn it back?
Isaiah 14:27 esv

....

Holy God, You have purposed to complete Your work in me. This fact reassures me even on nights when everything around me is topsy-turvy.

Humanly speaking, there is often chaos in my life, not because of sinful deeds, but because of the many facets of living on this earth. I can get caught up in my responsibilities and become anxious when I'm not accomplishing my own goals.

Help me to remember that You also have goals for me! And You have perfectly good goals, not the unreasonable ones I sometimes set for myself. Your goals include that I would be perfectly conformed to the image of Your Son and that I would live in holy relationship with You and with others around me.

As I think about Your goals before I drop off to sleep, I celebrate Your purpose that is higher and better and holier than anything I can dream.

I accept whatever You have for me.

In Jesus' name, amen.

THE JOY OF REVELATION

So brace up your minds; be sober (circumspect, morally alert); set your hope wholly and unchangeably on the grace (divine favor) that is coming to you when Jesus Christ (the Messiah) is revealed.
1 PETER 1:13 AMPC

....

O Lord, one of the most glorious things about knowing You is the increasing revelation of Your nature and character. As I've spent time in Your Word and in fellowship with You, I've been drawn ever closer to You, to the holy aspects of Your nature.

When Jesus walked on this earth, I believe others were drawn to Him because of the traits He exhibited even before they heard Him teach. The Godhead, three in one, is holy and pure and loving and welcoming through the atonement of Christ. This truth about You has gladdened my heart over and over again.

Many times, non-Christians believe that following Christ means choosing a hard taskmaster. But that's just another of the devil's lies. Following You means submitting myself to the one who loves me completely and continues to reveal Himself to me in increasingly meaningful ways.

Thank You, Lord, for being my loving master and friend and so much more!

Amen.

MEDITATION ON HIS REDEMPTION

May my meditation be sweet to Him;
as for me, I will rejoice in the Lord.
PSALM 104:34 AMPC

. . . .

Dear Father, thank You for making Yourself known to me through Your Word and through the testimony of others. Thank You for sending Jesus to live on earth and leave an example for me. Tonight, I'm meditating on how different my life is because of You and marveling that You wanted me to be in Your family.

You didn't have to plan my redemption. Long before I was born, You could have decided to annihilate mankind and start over. But You looked ahead, down through the millennia, and wanted to give Your creation a chance to choose You and experience forgiveness and restoration. What cost to You on Calvary! What expense to You in the suffering of Your Son! Yet, You were willing, and now I am the recipient of Your saving grace!

My last thoughts of the day will be of You and Your love. I'm unworthy, yet You have made me worthy. How great You are! Take my life and let it be a sacrifice back to You until I see You face-to-face in glory.

I love You, Lord. Amen.

The Gifts of Sleep

KNOWLEDGE OF MY GOD

*But grow in grace (undeserved favor, spiritual strength)
and recognition and knowledge and understanding
of our Lord and Savior Jesus Christ (the Messiah).
To Him [be] glory (honor, majesty, and splendor)
both now and to the day of eternity. Amen (so be it)!*
2 PETER 3:18 AMPC

. . . .

Father God, thank You for calling me to Yourself. Thank You for making me part of Your family. Thank You that I can grow in knowledge of You. As I get ready to sleep tonight, I know I'm on my way to heaven and You are helping me to mature in my spiritual understanding.

I'm reminded that all I need to do as Your child is take advantage of the opportunities to grow. I must get spiritual nourishment by reading Your Word and meeting with other believers and listening to good preaching and good music. I need to talk to You every day so our relationship can stay vibrant and current. And I must be attentive to the voice of the Holy Spirit when He tells me something I need to do or something I shouldn't do.

My growth in knowledge will be the result of my obedience and my ongoing passion to know You better. Thank You that I can sleep tonight assured that You want me to grow!

Amen.

THE UNDERSTANDING OF TRUTH

And we know that the Son of God has come and has given us understanding, so that we may know him who is true; and we are in him who is true, in his Son Jesus Christ. He is the true God and eternal life.
1 JOHN 5:20 ESV

. . . .

Dear Lord, I know there's a difference between knowledge and understanding. Knowledge is head based, and it is necessary. Understanding is the practical application of that knowledge, and it's a gift God gives us as we walk with Him.

I want to grow in my understanding of Your ways and purposes. I want to be open to new light from Your Word. I want to be teachable as I learn from my brothers and sisters in Christ. The Bible speaks of people who grew and increased in understanding. I want that to be said of me. On that day when I stand before You, I know I won't have perfect understanding, but I want it to be the best it can be. I want You to be able to say, "Well done," to me.

Lord, my heart is open to Your leading, and I'm determined to be obedient to what You show me. I look forward to what I will learn tomorrow as You lead me in Your way.

Amen.

THE RICHNESS OF WISDOM

*I do not cease to give thanks for you, remembering
you in my prayers, that the God of our Lord Jesus
Christ, the Father of glory, may give you the Spirit of
wisdom and of revelation in the knowledge of him.*
EPHESIANS 1:16–17 ESV

....

Lord God, when I think of wisdom, I remember the story
of Solomon that I learned in Sunday school. You told him
that he could ask anything of You, and he asked for wisdom
and not wealth. His request pleased You, and You gave him
wealth anyway.

In Your Word, wisdom is actually wealth. It is a kind of
riches that many lack. But those who have it are blessed
beyond measure.

I ask that You would grant me wisdom in all its richness
and reward. Let me not be a flighty, silly woman who is only
concerned with the current fads of this temporal world.
Rather, let me be a woman who values eternal things and
who seeks wisdom.

As I prepare to rest for tonight, I know I can trust my
future to You, and I can also trust my decisions to Your
wisdom. I'm depending on You for my tomorrows!

Amen.

THE PRACTICALITY
OF DISCERNMENT

*These things we also speak, not in words which man's
wisdom teaches but which the Holy Spirit teaches,
comparing spiritual things with spiritual. But the
natural man does not receive the things of the Spirit
of God, for they are foolishness to him; nor can he
know them, because they are spiritually discerned.*
1 CORINTHIANS 2:13–14 NKJV

. . . .

O Lord, I'm glad You're working a spirit of discernment
in me. Before I knew You, I didn't think too deeply about
spiritual things, but now I know that this part of life is the
most important.

As I study Your Word, I'm amazed at the things I learn
about You. Thank You for my pastor who teaches me from
Your truth. Thank You for my small group or class in which
I learn how to live out Your Word in practical ways. Thank
You for my Bible study group and my Christian friends and
my many brothers and sisters in Christ—these blessings
support me and encourage me.

As I face a new day tomorrow, I know that I'm on a jour-
ney of learning with You. I know I can put my hope in You.

In Jesus' name, amen.

THE BLESSING OF HONESTY

But we have renounced disgraceful, underhanded
ways. We refuse to practice cunning or to tamper
with God's word, but by the open statement
of the truth we would commend ourselves to
everyone's conscience in the sight of God.
2 CORINTHIANS 4:2 ESV

. . . .

O God my Father, one of the joys of living for You is the blessing of living an honest life. This does indeed help me to sleep better! I don't have to worry about others finding out that I've lied to them. I don't have to be anxious about keeping all my stories straight. I don't have to be fearful that my family or friends will discover I'm not who or what I claim to be. I can go to sleep without angst, resting in Your perfect peace.

As I commit myself to sleep, knowing that You are in control, I'm thankful for the ways You show me to walk in truth with others and before You. When I stand before You someday, I want nothing to be hidden, no secrets I haven't dealt with, no covered-over sins I refused to confess.

Thank You for helping me to live honestly.

In Jesus' name, amen.

THE PRACTICE
OF COMPASSION

*Finally, all of you be of one mind, having
compassion for one another; love as brothers,
be tenderhearted, be courteous.*
1 PETER 3:8 NKJV

. . . .

Lord Jesus, tonight I'm wanting to focus on the spirit of compassion that You want to develop in me. I know that as a child of God, I'm called to have compassion for those around me. This means You're working on my natural inclination to think of self first and others second. You're awakening in me an awareness that I must deny myself (refuse to gratify myself first) and instead honor You by deferring to others.

Compassion is what I usually think of when I see a homeless person sleeping under a bridge or an intoxicated person staggering down the street. I know we're to have compassion on the lost and sinful people around us who need Jesus. But I'm understanding more and more that I am to have compassion on my fellow Christians as well, because they're in a process of learning just like me and have their own areas of natural weakness and temptation. All of us have areas of our lives that we want to see changed by the power of the Holy Spirit. As I go to sleep tonight, I resolve to practice compassion in the morning.

Amen.

A SPIRIT OF GENTLENESS

You have also given me the shield of Your
salvation; Your right hand has held me up,
Your gentleness has made me great. You enlarged
my path under me, so my feet did not slip.
PSALM 18:35–36 NKJV

Heavenly Father, the spiritual trait of gentleness is one that I want to have in greater measure. In this psalm, David is extolling You for how Your gentle love has worked in his life. And one of the fruits of the Spirit is gentleness. This is an important characteristic of a follower of Christ.

I can't work gentleness in myself, but as I stay connected to You, You will grow this grace in me. Gentleness does not mean, however, that I will have no backbone. No, indeed, I will be strong in my commitment to You and to spiritual disciplines. Gentleness simply means that I won't be harsh or uncaring in my attitude and that I will reflect the shepherd heart of my Lord in my dealings with others.

When I start my day in the morning, I know I can trust You to be at work in me, prompting me when I need to exhibit more gentleness. Thank You, Lord, for caring about my spiritual progress and cultivating spiritual fruit within me.

Amen.

A LIFE OF FRUITFULNESS

*You did not choose Me, but I chose you and
appointed you that you should go and bear fruit,
and that your fruit should remain, that whatever
you ask the Father in My name He may give you.*
JOHN 15:16 NKJV

. . . .

Dear Lord, You have appointed me to bear spiritual fruit,
and I want to do that well. Truthfully, I usually have trouble
seeing the Spirit's fruit in my life; but once in a while, I recognize that I have a changed nature and changed desires.
Sometimes others tell me about the difference they see in
me, and that encourages me too.

As I go about my day tomorrow, I want others to look
at my life and see that You are my master. I don't want
to be a bearer of fruit that doesn't mature or ripen. I want
to be a bearer of fruit that comes into full bloom with all
its color and sweetness.

I ask You, Lord, to prune the branches of my life and
give me a heart that trusts in the gardener. I will go to sleep
tonight secure in the knowledge that You do all things well.

In Jesus' name, amen.

THE SINGLE PURPOSE
OF DEVOTION

*I beseech you therefore, brethren, by the mercies
of God, that ye present your bodies a living
sacrifice, holy, acceptable unto God, which is your
reasonable service. And be not conformed to this
world: but be ye transformed by the renewing of
your mind, that ye may prove what is that good,
and acceptable, and perfect, will of God.*
ROMANS 12:1–2 KJV

. . . .

Lord of all, tonight I say again that my life is Yours. You
are the master of me. I want my life to be marked by devo-
tion to You. When I'm tempted to snatch back the sacrifice
from the altar, convict me, Lord.

A devoted life is one that is lived for a single purpose.
I want that to be said of me. And I know You can help
me live out that kind of life. When I think of the coming
week and how You have promised to go into it with me,
I feel like rejoicing. Lord, a life devoted to You is the happiest life possible. I have no need to fear anything that
can happen on this earth, because all things are held in
Your hands.

Tonight, I renew my commitment to present myself as
a living sacrifice to You. Not a dead one, but an alive one
who will gladly do Your will tomorrow when I awaken.

Amen.

AN EXAMINATION
OF MY BEING

Search me, O God, and know my heart: try me,
and know my thoughts: and see if there be any wicked
way in me, and lead me in the way everlasting.
PSALM 139:23–24 KJV

. . . .

Lord God, nothing can be hidden from You.

Tonight, search me and know me. You already know if there is anything untruthful in me, anything dishonoring to You, anything from which I need Your cleansing. But I want You to show me the results of Your examination of my soul. Reveal to me where I need to mature in my knowledge and understanding of You. Show me how I can grow in my obedience and service to You.

Since I'm human, I know I'll need to grow in grace until I get to heaven. But I do want to increase my surrender so that I will be more sensitive to Your voice and these discovery sessions won't be so intense.

Thank You, Father, for looking into my life and helping me to live a life of truth before You.

Amen.

BEAUTIFUL WORSHIP

Give unto the LORD the glory due unto his name;
worship the LORD in the beauty of holiness.
PSALM 29:2 KJV

. . . .

Lord of heaven, before I slip under the sheets tonight, I will give glory to Your name.

You are the ruler of heaven and earth. You are the maker of all things. You are the redeemer of humankind. You are the King of kings and Lord of lords. You are the Messiah and the coming conqueror.

I want to fall down before You and tell You that I am Your servant, Your follower, Your child. You are the great Lord of heaven and earth, and yet You choose to love me and care for me and give me an eternal home with You. My life is an offering of gratitude back to You. And tomorrow, as I rise to face a new day that You have given me, I will rejoice in the knowledge that You are the sovereign master of it all—and yet You gave Your life to redeem me from sin. Thank You, Lord Jesus.

I love You. Amen.

AN ANTHEM OF PRAISE

I will praise the LORD as long as I live; I will sing
praises to my God while I have my being.
PSALM 146:2 ESV

. . . .

Heavenly Father, I come before You at bedtime to praise
You again for who You are and what You have done. You
have been my guide and friend today, my sustainer and
redeemer. I will praise You because You are the very reason
for my existence. From before my conception, You knew
about me. You planned this day for me before I even drew a
breath. And now, here, this night, I know You as Savior and
Lord. What an amazing God You are!

I want my life to be an anthem of praise back to You.
While I go about my daily tasks, I want the words I say and
the deeds I do and the way I dress and conduct myself to
speak for me about the one I belong to, the one I serve with
every fiber of my being.

Without You, I can do nothing. My plans are worthless
on their own. My eternity is bleak unless I have You. And so
tonight, God of my days and nights, I praise You!

Amen.

COURAGE FOR THE BATTLES

*Wait for the LORD; be strong, and let your
heart take courage; wait for the LORD!*
PSALM 27:14 ESV

. . . .

Lord Jehovah, I know I can look to You for courage for
my days. There is never a challenge that You can't meet.
Your strength is made perfect and complete in my human
weakness. This weakness is not one of willful sin but of
human frailty. I simply am not able to fight off the attacks
of the enemy, but You are. Like the little children's song
says, "I am weak, but You are strong."

As I fluff my pillow and pull back my quilts, I turn
to You for help with all the battles I will face tomorrow. I
rely on You to give me courage just as You gave courage
to a shepherd who stood up to fight a giant. He knew
that the battle was Yours, in Your name, for Your honor. I
know the same. Whatever Satan may throw at me tomorrow will be an insult against You, for he loves to attack
Your children.

But You are greater and stronger, and You will be tri-
umphant. All I have to do is trust and obey.

Thank You, Father, for the gift of courage. I take comfort
in Your strength tonight.

Amen.

A REASON FOR HOPE

Blessed be the God and Father of our Lord Jesus Christ! According to his great mercy, he has caused us to be born again to a living hope through the resurrection of Jesus Christ from the dead.
1 PETER 1:3 ESV

. . . .

Dear Father God, hope is what the world needs, and hope is what You bring. There is no part of this earth that You cannot enliven and infuse with hope. The only condition is that we must put our trust in You and surrender our ways of working things out to You. When we do, we find that we gain a living hope through the resurrection of Jesus Christ from the dead.

For if Jesus can rise from the tomb, He can do anything. His power can change the circumstances I face and those of the entire world.

Tomorrow, I may face unusual questions or problems; I may have a run-in with a skeptic. But I must remember that deep down in every human being is a desire for hope. And I know the source of hope. Give me opportunities and wisdom to share the reason for my hope. And thank You for being my living hope!

Amen.

THE REWARD
FOR ENDURANCE

*For you have need of endurance, so that when you have
done the will of God you may receive what is promised.*
HEBREWS 10:36 ESV

. . . .

God, my Father, I want to live my life with endurance. It
would be pointless for me to start well and then slack off
before I reach the finish line. Fair-weather disciples don't
claim the prize. Those who make it to the goal have determined in their hearts to make it, and they put forth the
continued effort to get there. They don't allow themselves
to be distracted by the culture or the scoffers or the glitz of
material possessions. They fix their eyes on the promise of
eternity with You and never quit.

Tomorrow is a new day. Thank you for Your help today;
and now that it is past, please guide my steps tomorrow.
Thank You for promising me grace and strength in measure
with the spiritual challenges I will face. Infuse me with hope
as I awaken in the morning and keep me grounded with an
eternal perspective. May Your kingdom be my first priority
and Your glory my ultimate desire.

I ask these things in the precious name of Jesus. Amen.

THE CONTINUITY OF SURRENDER

Submit yourselves therefore to God.
Resist the devil, and he will flee from you.
JAMES 4:7 ESV

. . . .

Father in heaven, one of the hardest things for me to do is to surrender my will. But You ask me to do this in an act of consecration to You. And You ask me to do it daily, in a thousand small ways, to continually affirm that I am not my own but under the control of the Holy Spirit.

This verse says that if I submit to or come under Your authority by surrendering my will to You, You will help me resist the devil and the temptation to make myself the boss of my life. That is always his way, to make me feel as though I should be calling all the shots. But the truth is that I'm not smart enough or wise enough to handle him. And so I rest in You and surrender my will and my ideas to You. You can show me the best course of action. You can direct my response. I am totally Yours.

As I sleep tonight, Lord, keep me in the safety of Your care. And please renew my spirit in the morning as I consecrate it to You.

In Jesus' name, amen.

THE CHOICE TO TRUST

*As for God, His way is perfect; the word of the LORD
is proven; He is a shield to all who trust in Him.*
2 SAMUEL 22:31 NKJV

. . . .

God of heaven and earth, the trust I have in You is for life.
You have called me by name and set Your loving eyes on
me. You sent Your Son to pay the penalty for my sin. You
raised Him to life on the third day in triumph over sin and
death. Because I trust in You, both present victory and
future victory are mine.

I can't get to heaven on my own, but You know the
way. And I know that, someday, You will lead me to that
glorious place where I will see You face-to-face and enjoy
Your presence forever.

As I live in fellowship with You on this earth, I daily put
my trust in You for everything from the clothes I wear to the
vacations I take to the amount in my retirement account.
You are the one I trust, my all in all. Your ways are perfect,
and Your Word is proven.

Thank You for the gifts that come to me because I
choose to trust in You. Give me a heart that trusts even
more as I go through the rest of my week.

I love You, Lord. Amen.

The Contentment of Sleep

BLESSED WITH PLENTY

*And ye shall eat in plenty, and be satisfied, and praise the
name of the LORD your God, that hath dealt wondrously
with you: and my people shall never be ashamed.*
JOEL 2:26 KJV

. . . .

God of my praise, I know I can praise You in every circumstance of life—the good and the bad. Today, I bring You my celebrations. I have plenty to eat. I have nice clothes to wear. I have a vehicle to take me places. I have family members who support me. I have a job that provides me with funds to live. I have friends who encourage me. I have lots of gadgets that make my life easier in the kitchen and laundry room and computer room. I'm blessed with so much, and I don't want to forget that it all comes from You. You are the giver of all good things.

I don't know what tomorrow will bring. You may decide that I can best serve You tomorrow with less. That was the story with Job. And he didn't even know the reason. But You were there for him, and You will always be there for me.

Thank You, Lord, for all the stuff and people I have in my life. I want to be thankful for everyday blessings!

Amen.

BEARING LOSS

*And [Job] said, Naked (without possessions) came I
[into this world] from my mother's womb, and naked
(without possessions) shall I depart. The Lord gave
and the Lord has taken away; blessed (praised and
magnified in worship) be the name of the Lord!*
JOB 1:21 AMPC

. . . .

O Lord, my God, loss is one of the most difficult places in
which to practice contentment. It's natural to grieve loss. In
the biblical story of Job, he mourned deeply, putting ashes
on his head, tearing his clothing, bowing to the earth in
sorrow. Yet, he continued to worship You and trust in You.

Bearing loss is a reminder of the curse upon this world—
the curse of sin. Every time we encounter a death or divorce
or house fire or tornado or debilitating disease, we are
reminded that decay and destruction stalk this earth and
everything in it.

Still, in our losses, we can turn to You, receive Your
comfort, and experience Your keeping grace.

Tonight, I commit my life and its losses into Your keeping. Sustain me in whatever I face, I pray.

In Jesus' name, amen.

BEING ALONE

I am like a desert owl of the wilderness,
like an owl of the waste places; I lie awake;
I am like a lonely sparrow on the housetop.
PSALM 102:6–7 ESV

. . . .

Dear Father God, in the beginning, You said it was not good for the man to be alone. And after You created the woman and brought her to the man and there began to be more people on the earth, one of the worst states in which to find oneself was that of being alone. It's true that some people are introverts and loners by choice; but even still, most of them enjoy family and a friend or two. But to be truly alone, without a friend or anyone with whom to talk or share experiences, is a difficult burden to bear.

It sounds as though the psalmist knew about that. Under the inspiration of the Holy Spirit (who knew that all of us would be reading this someday!), he described two very lonely animals in bleak settings and likened himself to them. I've felt this way at times too.

Father, I know that even when I'm alone in a human sense, I am never far from Your presence. Help me to practice contentment tomorrow by offering my loneliness back to You and watching how You redeem it.

In Jesus' name, amen.

SERVING A FULL HOUSE

She rises while it is yet night and provides food for
her household and portions for her maidens.
PROVERBS 31:15 ESV

O Father in heaven, there are times when instead of being alone, I feel I'm surrounded by too many people. This doesn't happen often; but when it does, I have to remind myself that I am there to serve and not to be served.

Not only is the woman of Proverbs 31 industrious, but she must be a morning person too. She rose while it was still dark outside! That's hard for me to do, so I'm glad it's not commanded. But I do want to take to heart the admonition about getting up early enough to do what needs to be done.

Despite all the talk of liberation and glass ceilings and other such topics, women have a God-given pull toward hostessing when guests are in the home. Men want to care well for guests too, but they don't seem to get as uptight about it as women nor face the upheaval in the same way.

Lord God, help me to be content when I have guests—content to serve as I would serve You.

Amen.

ACCEPTING A CRUSHING BLOW

To you, O LORD, I call; my rock, be not deaf to me,
lest, if you be silent to me, I become like those who
go down to the pit. Hear the voice of my pleas for
mercy, when I cry to you for help, when I lift up
my hands toward your most holy sanctuary.
PSALM 28:1–2 ESV

Mighty Father, you are my rock. I trust in You when my life seems to be in pieces. I don't know all the details of Your will, but I do know that You have planned for me to be holy and perfect and have promised to weave all things into a beautiful pattern for good.

When life crushes me with its blows, hold me fast. Don't let the storm extinguish Your light in me. Help me to practice the grace of acceptance in the loss and grief I face. It might be a little thing, or it might be very big. Either way, You are there beside me through it all because I am Your child.

There are examples throughout scripture and down through history of Your people who have endured life disappointments with a kind of holy surrender. I want to do the same.

Thank You for Your great provision for me. I trust You for tomorrow.

Amen.

COMMITTING TO FORGIVENESS

*Then Peter came up and said to him, "Lord, how often
will my brother sin against me, and I forgive him?
As many as seven times?" Jesus said to him, "I do not
say to you seven times, but seventy-seven times."*
MATTHEW 18:21–22 ESV

. . . .

O Lord, thank You for the strength You give me to fulfill Your Word. It's hard to practice contentment when someone has wronged me, betrayed my confidence, taken advantage of me, or slighted me. The easiest thing to do is simply to ignore and purposefully stay away from that person. But that's not what You want me to do.

When someone has acted against me, the best thing for me to do is to forgive and keep on going. You offer the grace to make this response a reality.

I lie here in my bed, Lord, and think about tomorrow and commit in my heart to forgive anyone who needs forgiveness from me tomorrow. At times, even my family misunderstands me and my motives. Even so, help me to remember that I need not worry about that. I just need to honor Your Word in this area, and You will do the rest.

Amen.

CARRYING A GRIEF

I am utterly bowed down and prostrate;
all the day I go about mourning.
PSALM 38:6 ESV

Father God, in this earthly life, death is one of the effects of sin's curse. Your Word tells me that all of us have an appointment with death. Unless You return in the clouds for me, I will go that way too. Tonight, I'm thinking of the loss of family and friends through death. I'm grieving those who are no longer with me. I know that those who trusted in You are safe in Your home, but the separation from them is difficult for me. I long to see them again.

I ask that You would help me as I grieve, to do so in hope and in recognition that death is a defeated foe. On the third day, at an empty tomb, Jesus claimed the victory over death and He will raise up all those who die in the Lord.

As I go to sleep tonight, I can smile as I remember that, someday, because I too have trusted in Jesus, I will go to that forever land where death will be no more.

Thank You, Lord. Amen.

REMEMBERING TIMES
OF CELEBRATION

*You shall have a song as in the night when a holy
feast is kept, and gladness of heart, as when
one sets out to the sound of the flute to go to the
mountain of the LORD, to the Rock of Israel.*
ISAIAH 30:29 ESV

. . . .

Holy Father, I love a good celebration. Whether it's a family reunion, a wedding, a holiday gathering, a church event, or something else that brings people together, it's a blessing to be able to come together with others, eat good food, and share laughter and stories. When we celebrate God's goodness as a corporate body, the sentiments are more meaningful and the joys are higher. The memories stay with us throughout our lives, and we're able to look back on that time as a landmark.

I know that not all of life is a feast day. There are also days of mourning and sadness as well as days of routine and monotony. But I'm thankful for the high-tide times in my year. They are a gift from You. Tonight, as I think about my life and the special times of celebration, I know that You are worthy of all my praise and thanks for the countless good things that come from Your hand.

Thank You, Lord. Amen.

WORKING IS FOR MY GOOD

Also that everyone should eat and drink and take pleasure in all his toil—this is God's gift to man.
ECCLESIASTES 3:13 ESV

Father in heaven, because You have given me the physical ability to work and provided a job for me to do, I praise You for the rewards of that labor. Thank You that I have learned the value of honest toil and that I have been taught the biblical principle that those who want to eat should work! Society functions better and You are glorified when each of us takes personal responsibility to provide for what we need with the means You give us. There are various ways of fulfilling that responsibility, but it's important that we do it.

Going to sleep at night means thinking about the time when I need to get up the next morning. Help me to rise with a spirit of gratefulness for my job, whether it's working within my home or outside of it. Help me to be not a complainer but rather an encourager to those around me.

All good things come from You, including work, for it was created when the first man and woman were in the perfect garden. And today, I still feel Your approval when I've done my best and have lain down to rest again.

Amen.

ACCEPTING THE GOOD AND THE BAD

Though the fig tree should not blossom, nor fruit be on the vines, the produce of the olive fail and the fields yield no food, the flock be cut off from the fold and there be no herd in the stalls, yet I will rejoice in the Lord; I will take joy in the God of my salvation.
HABAKKUK 3:17–18 ESV

Heavenly Father, I will praise You at all times—the good and the bad. It's easy to be happy when things are going well, but it's especially important for me to praise You when they aren't. My soul needs the discipline of realizing that You are good and that You are sovereign, whatever circumstance I'm in currently. My praise for You is not based on whether things are going well for me right now, but rather on Your holy character and mighty power and infinite love. These things do not change.

Thank You that today I have food to eat, clothes to wear, and a room in which to sleep. Thank You that I know You will never leave me. Thank You that You will bring me to the other side, and You will still be Lord.

Amen.

FEELING OVERWHELMED
WITH LIFE

*I cry to the Lord with my voice; with my voice to the
Lord do I make supplication. I pour out my complaint
before Him; I tell before Him my trouble. When my
spirit was overwhelmed and fainted [throwing all
its weight] upon me, then You knew my path.*
PSALM 142:1–3 AMP

O Lord, there are days when the pressures and stresses
of life are especially heavy. On these days, even simple
complications feel like major obstacles. Nothing tragic or
consequential may have happened; but the accumulation
of hundreds of tiny details adds up to a lot of weight. And
it's often difficult to explain this to others. My reasons for
feeling overwhelmed may not make sense to them.

Yet, I know that You understand perfectly. You know
my temperament, what speaks to me, what stresses me,
what comforts me. You know me better than anyone. And
so I bring to You my day tomorrow. Give me the grace You
know I need to cope with its demands. Let me not fall
apart but instead depend on Your divine empowerment
to accomplish Your will.

In Jesus' name, amen.

VALUING GOOD RELATIONSHIPS

A friend loves at all times,
and a brother is born for adversity.
PROVERBS 17:17 ESV

....

Lord God, thank You for the God-honoring and whole-some relationships You have brought into my life. Thank You for helping me to know Your truth so that I can invest in the right kind of relationships. When we orient our lives around Your Word, we are healthier and happier.

Today's verse says that those friends who really care about us will love us at all times, sticking by us when things go wrong and speaking truth to us when we need it. They won't be swayed by other influences but will love us through all seasons, even when it means sacrifice.

Help me, Lord, to be that kind of friend in my relation-ships. Show me how I can reflect You tomorrow as I interact with the people You've allowed me to befriend. Give me the discernment to tell when they need an extra phone call or when I need to pray a little more for them. May we encourage one another in Your way and be a blessing to one another all the days of our lives.

In Jesus' name, amen.

COPING WITH
DAMAGED FRIENDSHIPS

Faithful are the wounds of a friend, but the
kisses of an enemy are lavish and deceitful.
PROVERBS 27:6 AMPC

. . . .

Faithful Lord, thank You that I can depend on You when others fail. Thank You that there is no shadow of turning with You. Thank You that You are faithful to the end, in every season, in every situation.

As I try to sleep tonight, I'm remembering those times when I've been betrayed by a friend. One of the most hurtful things I've ever experienced was having someone I trusted turn on me and become almost an enemy. Perhaps the reason was a difference of philosophy or a difference of opinion on some point of theology or politics or parenting. But the reason wasn't enough, in my mind, to make us adversaries. I would rather still be friends with radically different opinions than be at odds in this way.

But, Lord, I must commit this situation to You, knowing that You know her so much better than I do and that You see all the reasons and complications. Please show her that our friendship doesn't have to be damaged this way. Please give me grace for tomorrow. Help me to be faithful in all the relationships You've entrusted to me.

In Jesus' name, amen.

FORGIVING MYSELF

*Therefore, [there is] now no condemnation (no
adjudging guilty of wrong) for those who are in
Christ Jesus, who live [and] walk not after the dictates
of the flesh, but after the dictates of the Spirit.*
ROMANS 8:1 AMPC

....

Abba Father, my conscience continues to assault me
and berate me and condemn me for sins of my past that
I have confessed to You. I can forgive others, but the
hardest person to forgive is me. I expect more of myself.
Or perhaps it's pride that can't accept that I actually did
something that needs forgiveness.

Help me to understand and embrace the fact that
when a sin is forgiven, I am no longer condemned. Show
me that I am a person too; and as such, I qualify for forgiveness from anyone involved (even myself). Implant
in my heart the message of this verse so that I can be
encouraged by Your truth. Purify my heart of any secret
longing for sin, and solidify my commitment to follow
You in ongoing obedience.

I ask these things in Jesus' name. Amen.

FORGIVING OTHERS

Bearing with one another, and forgiving one another,
if anyone has a complaint against another;
even as Christ forgave you, so you also must do.
COLOSSIANS 3:13 NKJV

....

Dear Lord, thank You for the forgiveness You offered me because of Calvary. I don't deserve Your mercy, but I'm so grateful You gave it. There was nothing I could do to atone for my offense against You. Even so, You freely forgave me because of Your Son's sacrifice. And You don't hold it over my head or ask me to prove myself. You wrote off the debt. Forever.

Now, Lord, I pray that You would give me the grace to practice that kind of forgiveness with others. When I'm wronged by someone else, help me to remember that I must forgive because Christ forgave me. It has nothing to do with the severity of the offense and everything to do with the forgiveness I myself have received. Forgiveness is not a feeling; it's a choice to release the other person from having to pay and to leave the result to You.

As I think about my week to come, I pray that You would enable me to forgive others.

In Jesus' name, amen.

RESISTING THE LIES

But You, O LORD, do not be far from Me;
O My Strength, hasten to help Me!
PSALM 22:19 NKJV

For He Himself has said, "I will never
leave you nor forsake you."
HEBREWS 13:5 NKJV

. . . .

Father God, there are times in my life when I feel alone, times when it seems You are far away, times when my prayers don't seem to reach You.

I know in my head that You are never far away, but my emotions get the better of my judgment at times, and I become anxious and fretful. Forgive me, Lord, for handling my feelings incorrectly in those times.

Your Word promises that You will never leave me nor forsake me. I'm so glad that You made this promise to those who put their trust in You. Now as I go through my week, help me to remember that my emotions can't be trusted. Sometimes the devil uses them against me, whispering his lies about You.

But I will trust in Your name and rejoice in the fact that You are constantly with Your children who bear Your name. I will lie down and sleep tonight, secure in Your steadfast love.

I love You, Lord. Amen.

BELIEVING TRUTH

The Lord will command His lovingkindness in
the daytime, and in the night His song shall be
with me—a prayer to the God of my life.
PSALM 42:8 NKJV

. . . .

Father, I know that You are my Creator. I know that You designed me for a purpose. But there are days when I feel so ugly and so useless that this negative self-perception overshadows my contentment. I long for beauty in my person and for gracefulness in my demeanor. I observe other women who seem not to struggle at all with the problems affecting me. They have clear skin and perfect teeth and healthy hair and a sense of poise and confidence. I'm sure they have their own struggles, but I don't see them.

Lord, I ask that You would remind me that You are always with me, that You love me, and that no matter how unwanted I feel, You made me the way I am on purpose and for a purpose. Anything less than perfect in me is the result of the sin and decay in this world. But in my essence, as You created me from the beginning, I am a witness to Your creative genius.

Thank You, Father, for hearing my prayer whenever I call to You.

Amen.

BOTTLING MY TEARS

You number my wanderings; put my tears into
Your bottle; are they not in Your book?
PSALM 56:8 NKJV

. . . .

Father in heaven, there are times when I feel like I can't stop the tears. Sometimes it's a big thing, and sometimes it's a little thing. Sometimes I'm grieving for someone else. Sometimes I'm grieving for me. Sometimes life just gets to be too much.

I know that there is a biological explanation for tears, but I also know they are an expression of deep emotion and are therefore an emotional reaction given to us by You, our Creator. And You understand them. Throughout scripture we read of people who experienced deep emotions, and You sustained them through all those complicated feelings. And because of that, I know You will sustain me too. I bring to You my tears and my heartaches and my problems that cause them.

I'm so thankful to have a God who loves me in every situation and wants to guide me in the right response. When You bottle up my tears over my lifetime, I know they will not outweigh the measure of Your love.

Thank You, Lord, for being my perfect Father.
Amen.

CONTEMPLATING TRANSFORMED DEATH

Have mercy upon me and be gracious to me,
O Lord; consider how I am afflicted by those who
hate me, You Who lift me up from the gates of death.
PSALM 9:13 AMPC

Holy Lord, since the fall of mankind in the garden of Eden, this earth has been under a curse. A curse of death. Everything decays and dies. Everything is on a collision course with death. No one will escape the effects of the curse by power or wealth or position. We all come into this world in the same way (naked), and we all go out in the same way (naked). We like to put off the effects of the curse for as long as we can by holding back the effects of aging, getting regular medical checkups, and so on. But in the end, we will succumb to its way.

Yet, for the Christian, the curse of death is redeemed through Jesus Christ. He won the victory over the grave. And He has closed His mighty hand around the keys of death, wresting them from the enemy and giving us the promise of eternal life. Lord, I won't let the fear of death rob my joy. You transform even the worst fear that man has.

Thank You, Lord. Amen.

NIGHT MEDITATING

*When I remember You on my bed, I meditate on You
in the night watches. Because You have been my help,
therefore in the shadow of Your wings I will rejoice.*
PSALM 63:6–7 NKJV

*My eyes are awake through the night watches,
that I may meditate on Your word.*
PSALM 119:148 NKJV

. . . .

Dear Father God, as I prepare for sleep tonight, my thoughts are drawn to Your greatness. I remember how You've helped me and how You've sustained me down through the years. When it's difficult for me to fall asleep, I've found that meditating on Your goodness is better than counting sheep. Your promises are true and everlasting. Your track record is flawless. Your people are blessed. Your words are absolute truth. Your plan of salvation is perfect. Your heaven is without comparison.

This world draws my attention away from You. It tries to lure me with its temporary pleasures. Only by keeping my mind fixed solely on You can I defeat the enemy's plan for my life. So to keep my mind focused on You even as I climb into bed, I will meditate on You and Your good works.

In Jesus' name, amen.

HOLDING ON TO THE RESURRECTION

*Jesus said to her, "I am the resurrection and the life.
He who believes in Me, though he may die, he shall live."*
JOHN 11:25 NKJV

. . . .

Eternal God, when I read a headline about a famous person
dying, I often ponder the sadness of the death of someone
whom many people will remember and who will be writ-
ten up in the history books but who, apparently from the
fruits of his life, did not know You. If that is true, then all
the accomplishments and awards and riches and influence
mean absolutely nothing. Those things have no value at
all when one is in hell and there is no hope of redemption.
How tragic.

But how different is the anticipation of the Christian.
Those who have cast their faith on Jesus Christ have the
same promise of the words He spoke to the sister of
Lazarus. He actually is the embodiment of life. If we have
Him, the Son, we have eternal life. It is His to give. And
all the things we do in service to our Lord are not lost but
will reap eternal rewards as others come to know Him
through our ministry.

Thank You, Father, for providing for my eternal hope.
In Jesus' name, amen.

EXAMINING A PASTOR'S RESIGNATION

But when He saw the multitudes, He was moved
with compassion for them, because they were weary
and scattered, like sheep having no shepherd.
MATTHEW 9:36 NKJV

. . . .

Dear Lord, when a pastor resigns, something more happens than just a move to another place of ministry. The congregation left behind goes through a grieving process. They go through a period of separation upheaval. They may even be a little angry with the pastor for leaving.

The Bible refers to pastors as *under shepherds*—shepherds who work for the Great Shepherd. And some of the traits of earthly shepherds also apply to ministry shepherds. Likewise, some of the traits of earthly sheep apply to spiritual sheep. For example, without a leader, sheep scatter. And so a pastor or shepherd will keep the flock from scattering over the countryside.

The decision to resign is a difficult one for a pastor and family, but at times it is God's will. I want to remember that, Father, the next time I encounter this situation. Help me to remember to pray for my pastor. And please give him a good week as he ministers to us.

In Jesus' name, amen.

CARING FOR FAMILY BROKENNESS

When my father and my mother forsake me,
then the LORD will take care of me.
PSALM 27:10 NKJV

. . . .

O Lord, sometimes my family misunderstands me. My extended family can't always be there for me. And though my parents love me, they are still human and can't always be with me. But You have promised to never leave me and to be with me even when my family can't or won't. I'm glad I have a caring family, but still it is wonderful to know that You are there regardless.

Many people today have disjointed and broken family relationships. Many little children don't know their fathers. Many teens have to move from Dad's house to Mom's house for visits. Many grandparents are raising their children's children. Many husbands and wives are going to bed alone tonight because divorce papers were served and they no longer have a marriage.

Lord, when I get up tomorrow and face my day, You may bring into it someone with a mangled family relationship. Help me to be sensitive to the hurt. And if You want me to say something, please help me to speak the words.

Thank You for being the God of the broken, the restorer of the wounded.

Amen.

AWAITING MEDICAL RESULTS

I would have lost heart, unless I had believed that I would see the goodness of the LORD in the land of the living. Wait on the LORD; be of good courage, and He shall strengthen your heart; wait, I say, on the LORD!
PSALM 27:13–14 NKJV

....

O God, my Father, one of the hardest things to do is to wait on medical test results. There is no way to guess what they're going to say. They take longer than we think they should. They're hard to read when they do come through. They come up before our minds when we try to eat or sleep or spend time with family. They always seem to be just a thought away, reminding us that we may not have long to live or that we may have to undergo unwanted treatments or that we may need drastic surgery.

Even so, I'm thankful for the medical advantages of modern life. Thank You that medical personnel can now catch diseases before they progress as far as they would have. Thank You that You give skill to surgeons and specialists to help us in those times when our bodies betray us. Thank You that You will give us grace in the hard times and courage when we need it.

Amen.

FILTERING NEWS REPORTS

*He is the radiance of the glory of God and the
exact imprint of his nature, and he upholds
the universe by the word of his power.*
HEBREWS 1:3 ESV

....

Father God, the news reports are discouraging. Evil men
are trying to snatch power. Politicians are corrupt. Morality
is almost an obsolete idea. Wicked ideology is increasing.
Education is suffering. Poverty and drug use are rising.
Cities are declining. Common sense is lacking. People are
dying and going into eternity without You. The universe
seems to be rocking and reeling. Scientists are declaring
that humans have damaged the planet and will bring about
their own demise. Wars are on the horizon as nation clashes
with nation.

But in the middle of this earthly chaos, Your Word rings
sure and true. Nothing will destroy this earth and cause
the end until You are ready. Your timetable is the one that
counts. While we need to be good stewards of nature and
its resources, You won't allow mere man to destroy Your
earth. You will continue to uphold this planet for as long
as Your will pleases.

Thank You for the confidence I have that You will keep
things going and that when the end comes, I will go to be
with You because Christ is my Savior.

Amen.

PRAYING IN THE WAITING ROOM

I lay down and slept; I wakened again,
for the Lord sustains me.
PSALM 3:5 AMPC

Lord, one of the most uncomfortable sleeping places is a hospital waiting room. Sitting and sprawling with all the other uncomfortable, worried families, a person has no real place to be alone, no good place to stretch out, and no change of clothes, refrigerator, or personal bathroom. I've tried, Lord, to do my best to be congenial and adaptable, but I usually sleep horribly in those conditions.

So, tonight, I want to pray for the families of patients in my local hospital, whether they're in the waiting room or the patient's room. Their nerves are tight, their hearts are hurting, their bones are aching, and their bank accounts are straining. I ask You, Lord, by Your power, to reach into those rooms and comfort their hearts. Send someone to show them the love of Jesus; and if You want that person to be me, please show me how to do that. Lord, hospital waiting rooms see some of the most heart-wrenching family drama, and only You know the amount of pain that those walls have seen. Cover those waiting family members with Your grace and love.

In Jesus' name, amen.

PREPARING FOR WAR

Though an army encamp against me, my heart shall not fear; though war arise against me, yet I will be confident.
PSALM 27:3 ESV

. . . .

Holy Lord, no army on earth can stop Your plan. I'm so glad for that. To have the reassurance that You are fighting my battles gives me faith and hope. Should the day ever come when an actual army is encamped outside my window, I will know where to turn.

In our world, Lord, nations invade and attack one another to further their power and increase their wealth. Neither of these goals is in line with Your will, because You tell us to be content with what we have! But these nations will continue to war until You come again as the conquering Savior and decide the outcome.

Lord, sometimes internal spiritual battles are as intense as those fought with physical weapons. I need to remember this principle that I don't have to fear when war rises against me; but rather, I can turn to You and be confident that You will win it for me.

I trust You for my battles tomorrow.
Amen.

SITTING BY A LOVED ONE'S BEDSIDE

*The LORD is near to the brokenhearted
and saves the crushed in spirit.*
PSALM 34:18 ESV

Dear God, my Father, a caregiver needs to be able to sleep almost anywhere, especially on a cot or in a recliner in the patient's room. If the situation is serious, the caregiver must stay close. But sleep is necessary for both the patient and the caregiver. And the emotional upheaval of watching a parent or loved one decline is an added detriment to good sleep.

At some point in my life, I'm sure I will be placed in this situation. Help me to remember then that You are near to the brokenhearted. Help me not to put undue pressure on myself for private devotions and long prayer times. Let me remember that I can pray as I serve, and that some seasons require different routines. Yet, let me not resist fellowship with You. I want the most difficult moments of my life to be marked by my relationship with the God of the universe.

I pray these things in Jesus' name. Amen.

PRACTICING HOSPITALITY

Use hospitality one to another without grudging.
1 PETER 4:9 KJV

. . . .

O God, hospitality is becoming a lost art—except for the magazine article kind where the house is styled for a photo shoot and looks welcoming in the pictures. Though there are some who do practice hospitality, there is such pressure to provide the perfect experience that many simply stay out of it altogether.

But Lord, I want to be a hospitable person who shares my blessings with others. Thank You for teaching me how important this is. I might not be able to give my guests the privilege of their own pillow and sheets, but I can provide the best You've given me and let them know that I care about their physical needs.

As I welcome others into my home, I pray that Your Spirit would enable me to interact well with them and to speak a word of truth as You prompt me. Thank You, Lord, for helping me in this little thing.

Amen.

SLEEPING AS I AGE

Cast me not off nor send me away in the
time of old age; forsake me not when my
strength is spent and my powers fail.
PSALM 71:9 AMPC

. . . .

God in heaven, since sin entered the world, decay and death have been present. Aging is part of the decaying and dying process. It's not a very happy thought, but I know it's true. And I try to take care of myself so I won't look older than I am! But still, I know that I am aging.

Part of the aging process involves sleep complications. Insomnia plagues many. So does excessive worry. And hormonal disturbances are another detriment to good sleep.

So, tonight, I pray first that You would help me as I age to accept the process while still keeping my youthful spirit and doing my best to care for my beauty as a woman of God should; and second, that I would be able to find a solution to sleep problems so that I can be at my best for You and my family during the day.

I know You hear my prayer, and I thank You for the answer already on the way.

In Jesus' name, amen.

GETTING GOOD NEWS

*Like cold water to a thirsty soul, so is good
news from a far [home] country.*
PROVERBS 25:25 AMPC

. . . .

Lord Jesus, thank You for the good news I received today.
It's something I've prayed for and believed for, and now
I'm celebrating Your gracious answer. Your love is always
amazing to me; and when something like this happens, I
know that You are the one behind everything perfect and
good. I know this good news is a gift from You.

After getting good news, I sometimes have trouble
sleeping because I'm so excited about the answer. A great
adrenaline rush comes from knowing that my God in
heaven hears and answers prayers! Thank You for letting
me see Your power once again.

Tonight, as I try to calm my emotions and get some
rest, I pray that You will be with those who don't have an
answer. Lord, be with the ones I know who are holding on
in faithful prayer day after day. Give all of us the grace to
pray in faith and then accept what You ordain. And help
us be able to sleep while we wait.

In Jesus' name, amen.

FEELING FORGOTTEN

*My kinsfolk have failed me, and my
familiar friends have forgotten me.*
JOB 19:14 AMPC

. . . .

Lord of heaven, when You walked the earth, You experienced what we do so that You could taste the full cup of humanity. I'm sure there were times when You felt forgotten and alone, distrusted and misjudged. Our family and friends may not mean to give us the impression that they don't care, but sometimes that's exactly the impression we get.

Being alone is a difficult burden. If I choose to be alone, that's one thing. But to be alone because I've been overlooked is painful.

Lord, help me remember that when I'm forgotten by others, I am right in Your sight. You have not lost track of me. You have not misplaced the blueprint for my life. You have not decided to spend Your time with someone who is more mature and better gifted. You are not a fair-weather friend.

Tonight, Lord, I will go to sleep with the assurance that You are everything I need. And when friends and family fail, You are always there!

Amen.

MANAGING PRAISE

*Everyone proud in heart is an abomination to the LORD;
though they join forces, none will go unpunished.*
PROVERBS 16:5 NKJV

....

Dear heavenly Father, we've talked about being forsaken
and forgotten and about difficult circumstances in life. On
the flip side, though, I recognize the spiritual danger of
receiving continual praise. The devil can use this anthem of
compliments against me, tempting me to become prideful.
All of us like to hear that we did something well. When our
performance is unusually good, we like to bask a bit in the
wonder of it as well as in the feeling of significance that
comes from others' applause.

But, Lord, help me not to imagine that I'm self-made or
that any of these compliments are mine. In reality, they are
Yours. I wouldn't have a brain to think with if not for You.
I wouldn't have arms and legs to carry out good deeds if
not for You. I wouldn't have the ability that allowed me to
impress others if not for You. It's certainly okay for me to
thank the compliment giver, but I shouldn't let their words
inflate my ego.

As I try to go to sleep at night, remove from my mind
the adoration of me and let me pass all the glory on to You.

In Jesus' name, amen.

LETTING GO OF A FRIEND

*Be of good courage, and He shall strengthen
your heart, all you who hope in the LORD.*
PSALM 31:24 NKJV

. . . .

Lord God, you made us for relationship, and friendships mean a lot to me. I come to You asking for grace to accept a recent change since my friend moved away. This transition is affecting my life on several levels, including the spiritual dimension. Help me to accept this change and make the best of it and support my friend in prayer as she tries to reach out in her new place.

Accounts of great friendships are recorded throughout the Bible, Lord Jesus; and when You walked on this earth, You had faithful friends who followed You as Your disciples and traveled with You and ministered with You. You understand the loss that is felt when a friend is gone. You experienced the deep betrayal of a friend when Judas became a traitor, focused on personal gain rather than godly relationships.

I ask tonight that You would give us both sleep—my friend in her new surroundings and me in my familiar ones. Let sleep be easy for us, and let us learn to glorify You in new ways.

In Jesus' name, amen.

CANCELING OUT A BAD MOOD

"Peace I leave with you, My peace I give to you; not as the world gives do I give to you. Let not your heart be troubled, neither let it be afraid."
JOHN 14:27 NKJV

. . . .

Father in heaven, thank You for the peace that You give freely to Your children. My peace started when I opened my heart to receive your forgiveness and trust in You for eternal life. Yes, I still deal with troubling situations in my life, and sometimes I feel one of those dark moods coming on. But I'm glad that I can turn to You and that You will help me in the moment I need You most.

I come to You tonight thanking You for Your perfect peace and praying that You would allow me to be a channel of that peace to others in our hurting world. Let me live with a joyful expression and open heart and willing hands. Bring me to people who need a peaceful word and prompt me to know when to speak it. Work Your will in me, one day at a time, one step at a time.

Thank You, Lord, for peace. Amen.

SHARING GOOD THINGS

*I will greatly rejoice in the LORD, my soul shall
be joyful in my God; for He has clothed me
with the garments of salvation, He has covered
me with the robe of righteousness.*

ISAIAH 61:10 NKJV

O God, this week has been a good one. I've followed in Your steps. I've been encouraged by Your people. I've learned new things from Your Word. I've rejoiced in Your provision for me. I've had meaningful conversations with my family. And I have seen You work in my life.

I wish every week could be like this, but it can't. I know there will be trying weeks ahead. But I also know Your grace and strength will accompany me into those weeks.

For right now, I want to praise You for my blessings. They are many. You've chosen to give me so many good things this week. Let me hold them with open hands. Let me share my plenty with others. Let me acknowledge that every perfect gift comes from You. And let me never take for granted the wonderful privilege of being Your child.

In Jesus' name, amen.

ASKING FOR TOTAL FILLING

And my soul shall be joyful in the LORD;
it shall rejoice in His salvation.
PSALM 35:9 NKJV

. . . .

Dear Lord, tonight I need an attitude adjustment so that I can live in contentment and praise to You. Some upsetting things happened at work today. This world is so godless, with people doing whatever pops into their heads. Coming home from that, I felt a need to detox, to rinse away the harmful, me-seeking attitudes and ingest the peace and joy of Your Spirit. Thank You that the Holy Spirit does come to dwell within us; and as I open my heart to His complete cleansing and filling, I will be empowered more than ever to live a life for Jesus.

As I drop off to sleep tonight, I lay my life and my attitudes and my tomorrow in Your hands and ask that You would make me a beacon of hope and light where You've placed me. Work out Your will for me and my family and the people we touch.

I want You to be central in every room of this temple that You indwell.

In Jesus' name, amen.

THINKING ABOUT HEAVEN

Then I, John, saw the holy city, New Jerusalem, coming down out of heaven from God, prepared as a bride adorned for her husband. And I heard a loud voice from heaven saying, "Behold, the tabernacle of God is with men, and He will dwell with them, and they shall be His people. God Himself will be with them and be their God. And God will wipe away every tear from their eyes; there shall be no more death, nor sorrow, nor crying. There shall be no more pain, for the former things have passed away."

REVELATION 21:2–4 NKJV

. . . .

Eternal God, my Father, thank You for preparing heaven for me.

Tonight my thoughts turn toward that perfect place that You are preparing. I don't need to worry that I won't like it or that I will be bored. I can trust You, the all-wise master designer. The place where I will spend eternity will be far greater than an earthly mind can grasp. That's why we'll need a new one, I guess!

Thank You for redemption.

Thank You for salvation.

Thank You for beckoning me ever forward in following You so that someday You can take me to Your eternal home.

These are the best nighttime thoughts of all.

I love You, Lord. Amen.

Scripture Index

OLD TESTAMENT

NEW TESTAMENT